The Battle of Britain

THE
BATTLE OF
BRITAIN

BY QUENTIN REYNOLDS

Illustrated by CLAYTON KNIGHT

RANDOM HOUSE · NEW YORK

The author wishes to express his thanks to the executors of the Estate of the late Sir Henry Newbolt, who have generously given him permission to quote four lines from the poem entitled "Drake's Drum" from *Poems New and Old* published by Messrs. John Murray of London.

THIRD PRINTING

To my nephew,

David Kirk

Contents

1	Churchill's Channel	3
2	Attack on a Convoy	12
3	Spitfires and Heinkels	22
4	A Trick That Worked	29
5	At Night Off the English Coast	37
6	Mission Accomplished	45
7	The Fliers at Biggin Hill	52
8	The RAF in Action	65
9	The Eagle Squadron	73
10	I Fly in an RAF Intruder	82
11	Rescue of a Pilot at Sea	91
12	London in the Blackout	98
13	The RAF Takes the Offensive	105
14	Another Mission Accomplished	116
15	Report of a Flight	125
16	Bombs Over London at Night	133
17	Plymouth	143
18	A City of Caves	152
19	England Could Take It	161
20	The Battle Is Won	170
21	Hope for the Future	175
	Index	179

The Battle of Britain

CHAPTER 1

Churchill's Channel

ENGLAND ISN'T VERY BIG. IF YOU LOOK AT YOUR
map, you'll see that it is an island about the size
of Minnesota or Idaho. Perhaps that is why, ever
since the beginning of time, greedy emperors
and kings have tried to invade and occupy little
England. The Romans invaded the island in
55 B.C., and they were later followed by the Vik-
ings and the Danes. But the last successful invasion of England was that of the Normans in
1066. In 1588, when the King of Spain sent the
famous Spanish Armada against the island, the

proud Spaniards were defeated by Sir Francis Drake. Napoleon, too, planned ways to conquer England, but he never succeeded in assembling the forces necessary for an invasion.

Boys in England are taught the history of their country at school. They know that they live on a small island which seems easy to conquer. They know, too, that there are only about forty-four million people living in England. Each one of these people loves his island and knows that some day he may have to fight to keep it free. It has always been that way and probably always will be.

Until 1940, all English boys wanted to join the Royal Navy. For a thousand years the British Navy had protected the island. Drake, Nelson, Beatty—these admirals were the great naval heroes of English schoolboys. Always the invading forces came by sea, and always the valiant British Navy was strong enough to beat them back.

In 1940 a new kind of invader tried to conquer England—the German Air Force, which was called the Luftwaffe. "Luftwaffe" is a German word that means "Air Force." Hitler had found it easy to conquer Poland, Czechoslovakia, Austria, Norway, France, and the other countries which fell to him one by one; he thought that England would be easy too. But Hitler was smart. He knew that the British Navy was too strong for his submarines and his heavy battleships like the *Bismarck*.

So Hitler tried to think of another plan. His many spies in England had told him that all the beaches of England were mined and strung with barbed wire. For a time Hitler thought of launching a huge invasion fleet across the English Channel, but his spies warned him that the British would fight until they died.

On August 1, 1940, Hitler knew that if he was going to strike at England, this was the time to do it. America wasn't in the war yet, although she was beginning to send airplanes and bombs and guns to England. However, many of the ships which started off from American ports were sunk by submarines. France had been crushed beneath the weight of German bombs and the power of German tanks. Yes, little England stood completely alone.

But she had a great leader—Winston Churchill. He looked somewhat like a bulldog, and he growled like a bulldog. But the people rallied around him when he spoke for them: "We shall go on to the end . . . we shall defend our Island, whatever the cost may be, we shall fight on the beaches, we shall fight on the landing grounds, we shall fight in the fields and in the streets, we shall fight in the hills; we shall never surrender. . . ."

Hitler couldn't believe this. He felt that the English, like the Americans, were trained for

peace—not for war. For almost ten years he had trained Germany for war. He thought that England would be easy.

So he decided to conquer England with his mighty air force—the Luftwaffe. "My Luftwaffe will bring England to her knees," he boasted. Hitler forgot that Kaiser Wilhelm had tried to bring England to her knees by attacking from the air. In 1917, during World War I, a squadron of German bombers (seventeen two-engined Gothas) attacked London. They dropped 128 bombs and killed 160 people. But this only made the English very angry. They fought back harder and harder, and one day, in November, 1918, Kaiser Wilhelm knew that he was beaten. But Hitler forgot how tough the English were.

Perhaps the attack on England looked easy because Hitler was so strong in the air. His air force was headed by Hermann Goering, who during World War I had been a fighter pilot in the famous Richthofen Squadron. But now Goering was too old to fly fighter planes. He directed the attack against England from Germany.

Goering had about 5,000 airplanes all ready to fly against England. What did the British have? Not much. They had lost about half of their Hurricanes fighting in the skies over France, but the RAF still had about 300 of them. And the new, fast little Spitfire was coming out of the factories, but there were only about 200 of them. What chance would they have against the mighty Luftwaffe? But then way back in 1588 it didn't look as though Drake had any chance against the Spanish Armada, either.

The Battle of Britain really began on Thursday, August 8, 1940. The opening guns were fired when sixty German dive bombers attacked a convoy of ships moving through the English Channel. The Germans thought it would be easy to bomb and sink the fifty ships in the convoy. Enemy planes crossed the English Channel at 5,000 feet, and thousands of people standing on the beaches at Dover and Brighton saw them coming.

But there was something else the crowd failed to see. Far above the German bombers a squadron of Hurricane fighters was patrolling at 16,000 feet—so high you couldn't see it from the ground. But each of the Hurricanes had a radio, and the pilots heard a calm voice coming through their earphones: "Bandits at 5,000 feet." (Bandits was the code word for German bombers.) At once the sixteen Hurricane pilots turned the noses of their planes down; they swooped down on the unsuspecting German bombers.

The people on the beaches saw them dive, and saw the flashes of light at the tips of the Hurricanes' machine guns. Then, above the heads of the crowd, German bombers started to tumble from the sky. Seven of them dropped flaming into the sea. Those that were not damaged dropped their bombs harmlessly into the Channel and hurried for home.

The leader of the Hurricanes, a great flier named Wing Commander Douglas Bader, watched the enemy turn tail. Bader had only one leg; the other had been shot off when he was flying with the RAF over France. Now he had an artificial leg and he could fly just as well as ever. When Bader saw the German bombers running for home, he radioed back to RAF headquarters. He said only four words, but when those words were printed in the newspapers the next day, all England felt a thrill of excitement. Bader had merely said, "It's still Churchill's Channel."

CHAPTER 2

Attack on a Convoy

PORTSMOUTH, ON THE ENGLISH CHANNEL, WAS one of the most important cities in England. Just as Norfolk, Virginia, is our big naval base, Portsmouth is the great British naval base. During the Battle of Britain, great numbers of warships and destroyers and submarines tied up at her docks. Behind the docks, there were factories and warehouses and arsenals. Every ship had to have ammunition for her guns, and gasoline and oil for her engines. Every sailor and every worker in the factories needed food. Many of these needed supplies came from the north of England, others had to be imported from other parts of the world.

Not everything which Portsmouth needed could be supplied from within England by train. Ships were loaded in the north and sent through the English Channel to Portsmouth. Others came from foreign countries. If they were sunk, there would be no ammunition for the guns, no food for the sailors and workers, no gasoline or oil for the engines. The Germans knew this. That's why the convoys of the ships in the Channel were the first targets of the German bombers during the Battle of Britain.

That Hitler himself was very much interested in stopping the Channel traffic became evident from one of his speeches. This speech, printed in the London newspapers, reported that Hitler had thundered, "The German Air Force dominates the English Channel."

I was a war correspondent in London at that

time, and my job was to find out if such reports were true. There was only one way to get an answer. I'd hitchhike a ride on one of the ships and find out.

The freighter on which I took passage was very small—but it could carry a lot of things that Portsmouth needed. We left late one afternoon and joined up with a convoy of thirty-nine other ships. Four gray destroyers escorted us. That didn't seem like much protection for forty ships, but each vessel in the convoy had anti-aircraft guns and machine guns on its deck.

As we started through the Channel, everything was very peaceful. I climbed to the mast of our ship, which was called the *Brighton* after a famous vacation town on the Channel something like our Atlantic City. We were the first ship in line. Looking back, I could see the other thirty-nine ships steaming along slowly and the four destroyers buzzing all over.

When we were about halfway through the Channel, I climbed down and stood with two sailors who were manning an anti-aircraft gun. Suddenly, the foghorn of our ship began to sound. That was the danger signal.

"Here comes Jerry," one of the sailors said cheerfully. The English had many names for the Germans. Usually when they heard German planes approaching they'd announce, "Here comes Jerry," as the sailor had done. I looked toward France, which lay to our left, but couldn't see anything.

I glanced at Simpson and the other sailor, whose name was Bill Kirk. The two were now rubbing their hands lovingly over the long barrel of the anti-aircraft gun. Then I looked up at the bridge where the captain stood. He knew that German planes were on their way to bomb this convoy. Yet he didn't seem a bit nervous as he leaned over the rail of the bridge, smoking his

pipe calmly. The English are like that. The more dangerous things become, the calmer they get.

Then we heard the planes. You nearly always hear them before you see them. I looked toward the French coast, but for a while I couldn't see them at all. When planes are flying low, they look dark and black. When they are flying high

they are silvery, because the sun is shining on them.

"There they are," Peter Simpson said, pointing almost directly above. He was right. There were sixteen of them flying very high, almost over us. Now they circled, and I felt they were preparing to dive at our little convoy. Our guns weren't firing, but I knew that on every one of our forty ships and on the four destroyers, men were looking through the sights of their anti-aircraft guns. The German planes were still too high to be fired at, but when they started to dive, our gunners would be ready. Our convoy kept right on steaming along in a straight line as though nothing were happening.

"I feel as if we're very much alone out here," I said to Peter Simpson.

"We're not alone," he said, chuckling. "Take a look there."

He pointed to the skies over the English coast, and I saw a wonderful sight. Twelve Spitfires were coming our way fast. I took my eyes away from them to look at the German planes, which had circled and now seemed to be coming at us. Then the Spitfires got close to them. You could hear the *da-da-da-da-da* of their machine guns and see the small golden flashes from the leading edges of their wings where the guns were.

A few minutes before, everything had been peaceful. Now it seemed as though the skies were filled with planes shooting at one another, diving, circling. Suddenly a puff of black smoke came from one of the German planes which was heading toward the French coast. I watched it and saw a glow in the tail. It was on fire. It had almost reached the coast when I saw what looked like four little dots drop from it. Big mushrooms seemed to open over the dots, and I realized then that the German fliers had bailed out. At that moment, their plane seemed to explode in mid-air. The German airmen floated down toward the Channel.

I borrowed Peter Simpson's glasses and looked toward the French coast. I could see a low, fast boat streaking toward the point in the water at which the Germans were about to land. This was the German sea-rescue squad.

Then there was the scream of a bomb, and I stopped watching the French coast. The bomb landed in the Channel about a hundred yards from our ship and exploded. It threw up a huge fountain of water, but that didn't hurt anyone.

Looking up, I saw three German planes start to dive at us. Now Peter Simpson and his pal bent over their gun. When the planes were within range they started to fire. They aimed at the nearest one. Little puffs of black started to appear around the German plane.

The other ships in the convoy were all firing now, and we had to shout to be heard. The sky was filled with little black puffs that hung there like small dark clouds. Our gun kept bang-bang-banging until the German plane they were aiming at was hit. Black smoke started to pour from its engines (it was a two-motored Heinkel), and it swerved away and headed toward France.

"That's one we won't have to worry about," Peter Simpson said, grinning.

CHAPTER 3

Spitfires and Heinkels

THE SPITFIRES WERE BUZZING LOUDLY NOW. Because they could fly higher and much faster than the bombers, they had the advantage. They'd get above them and dive at them with all their guns going. Then they'd swoop up again and do it all over.

The German bombers were now jettisoning their bombs. That means they were dropping them in order to lighten the load so they could dodge away from the Spitfires. The bombs fell harmlessly into the water, making a great deal of noise and sending up big fountains of water, but not hurting anyone.

Then suddenly all the German planes turned around and headed for home. They'd had enough. The Spitfires chased right after them. Two more German bombers were hit and we saw them burst into flames and go crashing into the Channel. The Spitfires chased the others to the French coast and then turned around and came back. A Spitfire could carry only enough gasoline to keep it going about an hour and a half. That is why the planes overhead were unable to follow the German planes any farther. They flew back and came down low over us, and everyone on all forty of our ships and the four destroyers waved his hat and cheered. Then the Spits, as they were called, disappeared over the English coast.

Now it was quiet again—just a peaceful summer day in the English Channel. The attack had

A Spitfire

lasted only ten minutes, although it had seemed hours, and not one of our ships had been hit. Our guns and the Spits had accounted for nine German planes in all.

A sailor came to tell me that the captain of our ship wanted to see me in the ward room. The ward room of an English ship, whether it's a big battleship, a destroyer, or a little freighter, is where the officers have their meals.

"Thought you might like a cup of cocoa," the

Captain said. The English like tea better than coffee, but cocoa is the Navy drink. It was thick, chocolatey cocoa.

"Will Jerry be back?" I asked the Captain.

"I hope so," he said simply. "That's the whole idea of this convoy. Do you know our code name? It's Bacon. We're the Bacon convoy."

"Why Bacon?" I asked, puzzled.

"Here in the English Channel the fishermen often use bacon for bait," he explained. "Well, we're bait. You saw those Spitfires come running as soon as Jerry came over us? They came from the Biggin Hill Airport. Now there are about twenty other airports behind the English coast. All of them are watching us. We're in constant touch with them by radio. Their Spitfires are all ready to take off at a moment's notice. We hope the German planes will keep coming after us. That will give the Spitfires a chance to destroy a lot of them."

"We're just the bait, then, that they are snapping at?" I asked.

"That's right." He smiled. "They may get two or three of us in the convoy, but our Spitfires will get an awful lot of them before the day is over."

"I read in the London papers that every time a convoy gets off the coast of Dover the big German guns start shelling the ships," I said. "Will they fire at us?"

"We hope so." The Captain took a long drink of the steaming hot cocoa. "We know those big German guns are somewhere around Calais on the French coast, but we haven't spotted their exact position. If they fire at us, the RAF planes will be up there spotting the flashes of the guns. Once they find out exactly where they are, our bombers will get over there and put them out of action."

"Are they very big guns?" I asked.

"The biggest ever made," the Captain said. "One of those shells would blow this ship right out of the water. . . . There's the alert. Here they come again. Come on up to the bridge to watch the fun."

This time there were thirty German bombers. But this time there were more Spitfires, too— twenty-four, to be exact. The fast fighter planes were on the bombers before they knew what was happening. They dropped their bombs all over the Channel but didn't hit a single ship.

We steamed on steadily at six knots. That's pretty slow, but in a convoy the slowest ship sets the pace for all the others. Some of our over-loaded ships could go only six knots an hour, so we all went six knots. I looked at the Captain, who was leaning over the rail of the bridge, puff-ing his pipe and looking straight ahead. He didn't even glance up at the fighting that filled the sky. This was an old story to him.

Eight of the German planes crashed into the sea. The others turned and ran for home.

After a few more puffs on his pipe, the Captain looked at his watch. "In a few minutes we'll be off Dover," he said, "and you know what that means."

I shook my head. "What does it mean, Captain?"

"Well," and he chuckled, "Dover on the English coast is just opposite Calais on the French coast, and Calais is where the big German guns are. They ought to start popping at us any minute. I know you don't want to miss that sight."

CHAPTER 4

A Trick That Worked

IT WAS COOL AND QUIET UP ON THE BRIDGE. THE Captain pointed to the French coast, twenty-two miles away.

"An American girl named Gertrude Ederle hopped into the water over there and swam all the way to Dover," he said. "She'd have a tough time swimming across the Channel now."

"I know Gertrude Ederle," I told him, feeling rather proud. "The water is pretty calm today. I'll bet if she were here she could do that swim all over again."

The Captain shook his head. "I'm afraid not," he said. "You forget that the Channel is filled with mines. We mine it on this side and the Germans mine it on the other side. As a matter of fact," he added, "we're going through a mine field right now."

"I don't see any mines," I told him.

"You're not supposed to," he said. "But you'll notice little flags bobbing up and down about every quarter of a mile. We're steering right between those flags. The flags show where the mines are floating just below the surface of the water."

While he spoke I glanced at Dover to the right. With its white buildings and its red roofs, it was a pretty town. In back of it rose the famous chalk cliffs gleaming white in the sun.

"Jerry is trying to swallow the Bacon convoy," the Captain said. "Look over there, just north of Calais."

I watched closely and saw a bright golden flash. A couple of seconds later, there was a dull boom. The big guns had started. Then, nearly half a mile ahead of us, a mighty fountain of water spouted up.

"That shell probably killed a lot of our Channel fish," the Captain said sadly.

"It looks as if their aim isn't so good, Captain," I said.

"The first couple of shells are just to get the range," he told me. He gave a sharp order to his helmsman. "Now we'll do a little zigzagging," he explained. "That may throw them off a bit. As a matter of fact, their aim is pretty good. Two days ago a convoy just this size went through here and six of the ships were hit. Those are the biggest guns ever made. They can shoot about twenty-five miles."

"Where are the planes?" I asked.

"They're so high up that you can't hear them,"

the Captain told me. "They've been up there for the past half hour just waiting for this. There are some fighters." He pointed over toward the French coast, and sure enough, there were four Spitfires high above Calais. "They're the spotters," the Captain said. "They're finding out just where those guns are. The flashes give them away. The Spitfires are radioing back to the bombers now to give them the exact position. There go the guns again."

There were two more bright flashes, two more muffled booms, and then we waited for the shells to land. Both landed harmlessly again in the water. But when they exploded, the shock was strong enough to rattle our little ship. For fifteen minutes the shelling kept up. Our convoy of thirty-nine ships kept right on following us, all zigzagging as we zigzagged. We'd go a hundred yards to the right and then turn sharply and go a hundred yards to the left. It seemed a miracle that none of the shells hit any of the ships.

"Now it's our turn," the Captain said. "Watch over there."

The four little fighter planes had disappeared, but now I saw a group of about sixteen British dive bombers glide over Calais. Then they swooped down, little silver streaks. Diving almost to the ground, they dropped their bombs and zoomed up again. One bright flash after another exploded back of the French coast. The British bombers dived again, and now our ears were filled with a "wumph" of bombs landing twenty-two miles away. But these were our bombs, and it was a pleasant sound because we knew they were falling near those German guns.

Then the British bombers turned back. They flew low over our convoy, and every one of them

waggled its wings in a friendly sign of greeting.

"Do you think they got any of the guns?" I asked the Captain.

"We'll know in a few minutes," he said.

It was quiet again. We waited, looking toward Calais, but we saw no more golden flashes and heard no more dull booms.

"They've tried to swallow the bait twice," the Captain said, "and twice they got hooked. If those guns hadn't been put out of action, they'd be firing at us now. Yes, it's been a good day.

We got at least a dozen of their planes and some of their big guns."

"It ought to be easy going from now on, Captain," I commented.

"We don't make port, you know, until the morning," he said, "and the Jerries' E-boats can be very nasty at night."

"What are the E-boats like?" I asked.

"Well," he said, "have you ever seen one of your American Coast Guard cutters? The E-boats are much like them. They're 103 feet long and they can go about fifty miles an hour. They carry heavy machine guns, and, what's more important, each E-boat carries two torpedoes. These darn E-boats are so fast that they can cross the Channel, fire their torpedoes, and be halfway home before we know what's happening. That is, they could before we had radar. Now at least we get a little warning."

"What's that?" I suddenly interrupted, pointing ahead. I could see what looked like six or seven speedboats slicing through the water, throwing up a lot of spray.

"That's our escort for tonight," the Captain said. "We'll need it, too, because this is going to be a bright, moonlit night. Those little motor torpedo boats all carry radar equipment. They also have powerful Isotta-Fraschini motors. And most important, they can throw smoke. If they spot any E-boats, they'll cover us with a smoke screen in about two minutes flat. And of course the RAF night fighters will be over us all night, just in case the German bombers want to take a crack at us."

"Then at least we won't be alone," I said in relief.

"No," and he smiled. "When you're in a British ship during wartime you're never alone."

CHAPTER 5

At Night off the English Coast

THE SIX LITTLE MOTOR TORPEDO BOATS REACHED us. Up close they weren't so little. They were about eighty feet long, sleek, and very low in the water. It was comforting to see the heavy machine guns on their decks. They throttled their engines down to keep pace with our slow speed.

Now the sun was beginning to set, a big orange ball dropping below the horizon. It was very quiet. It seemed as though the world had stopped breathing to watch our convoy.

"We might as well have dinner while it's

quiet," the Captain said cheerfully, and we went down to the ward room. Three other officers had dinner with us. It was a good dinner, much better than I could have had in London.

"They call the Navy the senior service," the Captain said. "That's because it's the oldest. There was an English Navy long before we ever had an English Army or an English Air Force, and because we're the senior service we get the best food."

That night we had steak and potatoes and beans and ice cream. And during dinner the Captain and his officers never mentioned the war. Instead, they argued about football. The English argue about football the way we in the United States argue about baseball. Their game of football is what we call soccer, and each year they have a World Series, just as we do.

While the officers and I talked and ate, the radio operator would come in every few min-

utes with a message for the Captain. There
were messages from the Admiralty (Navy headquarters) and from RAF headquarters. The
Captain read one of the messages and laughed.

"Amazing thing about radio," he said. "Here's
a message from London telling us that a heavy
fleet of bombers will pass over us in a few mo-
ments. The bombers are at thirty thousand feet,
which means that they're probably headed for
London or Coventry and won't bother with us.
These planes were probably picked up by radar
ten minutes ago. The news was flashed to RAF
headquarters in London, and now we know all
about them. Incidentally," he said, "there's
something else in this message. The RAF tells
me that Spitfires will be over us all night, flying
at sixteen thousand feet."

After dinner we went on deck. I could hear
the heavy beat of engines coming from the
French coast. These were the German bombers

the message had told us about. I hoped they wouldn't hit London too hard. Somehow I felt safer on the deck of this little trawler than I would have felt in London.

We were only about a quarter of a mile off the English coast now, and I knew we were passing towns and villages, but not a light showed. The towns were all completely blacked out.

Now the German bombers were directly above us. There is no need to be afraid of a bomber when it's overhead. After an airplane drops its bombs, they travel for a while in the direction in which the plane is going. They never drop straight down. But these German bombers weren't interested in us. The sound of their engines faded as they crossed the Channel over the English coast.

Then suddenly the whole English coast blazed with light. A hundred white shafts pierced the darkness over Dover. And the anti-aircraft guns opened up at the German bombers so high above. Now and then a German bomber would fly into the beam of one of these searchlights. At once a dozen other fingers of light would move toward it, trying to keep the plane spot-lighted until the anti-aircraft guns could get its range.

The coast, which had been so dark and quiet, was now exploding with flashes of light from the guns and from the noise of the shells as they burst four miles overhead. Occasionally there would be a sharp burst of light above us and we would know that an anti-aircraft shell had scored a direct hit. There would be one less German plane to reach London.

It was quiet again and the whole coast was in darkness. I walked up to the bridge with the Captain. One man sat beside some weird-looking instruments. He had earphones on his head.

"He's in charge of our anti-submarine detec-

tion instruments," the Captain said. "We call this the ASDIC. Did you raise anything yet, Bob?" he asked.

"Not yet, sir," was the answer. "It's a little early for them."

It was quiet for nearly an hour, and then we again heard the beat of engines. But these were RAF planes going toward France. As they approached the French coast, searchlights appeared from Boulogne and from Calais. There seemed to be hundreds of them. We couldn't hear the German anti-aircraft guns firing, but we could see the red and purple tracer bullets knifing upward, cutting across the dead white of the searchlight beams. It was like a wonderful display of Fourth of July fireworks, except that these weren't harmless rockets or Roman candles.

Then, just north of Calais, a British plane dropped a flare and a huge mound of gold light appeared.

"Smart, those RAF bombers," the Captain said, chuckling. "They destroyed those German guns this afternoon, all right, but they know that the Germans have probably rushed up fresh guns. They're probably installing them right now. But I'll bet those guns will never get a chance to fire."

Just then the British planes started dropping bombs at approximately the same point where we had seen the flashes of the big guns earlier in the day. The still night air carried the double-barreled sound of the bombs exploding. We could tell from the throaty wumph-wumph sound that these were very big bombs indeed. The shelling kept up for half an hour. We sailed along showing no lights (we couldn't even smoke on deck), hugging the friendly darkness of the Channel waters.

CHAPTER 6

Mission Accomplished

A VOICE BROKE THROUGH THE DARKNESS. "GET-ting an echo, sir," the man with the earphones said sharply to the Captain. (The ASDIC worked like this. It sent out sound waves and if the sound waves hit something like the hull of a ship they bounced back and made an echo.)

The Captain nodded calmly.

"It's getting stronger," the man with the ear-phones said.

The Captain turned toward his signalman, who had been standing alongside the heavy blinkers. During the day when one ship wanted to signal to another, it was done by signal flags. At night it was done with the blinkers.

"Tell them to give us some smoke," the Captain said, and the blinker began to flash the message to the motor torpedo boats. Within twenty seconds the little boats were streaking up and down. Heavy grayish smoke was pouring from their sterns.

"Whether it's submarines or E-boats, we'll give them a run for their money," the Captain said grimly.

"Suppose it's a submarine," I asked the Captain. "What could those little motor torpedo boats do against it?"

"Plenty," the Captain said. "You just saw six of the little MTB's. There are six more trailing us five miles astern. By now they have been warned and they're racing up to put themselves between us and the French coast. Each of those boats has four depth charges in its stern. If there is one thing a submarine is afraid of, it's a depth charge."

Now we could hear the full throaty roar of the powerful engines of the torpedo boats. We couldn't see them, of course, because the smoke had settled over us like a thick fog. A few

minutes later we heard four dull explosions, and we knew the depth charges were searching out the enemy submarines. Then we heard the sound of machine-gun fire. It sounded as though it were close to the French coast.

"Our boys have spotted some E-boats," the Captain said.

The machine-gun fire died away and we steamed on through the quiet night. Suddenly we heard one sharp explosion quite near.

"I'm not sure what that was," the Captain said, "but I think it was an E-boat that tried to sneak in. Only last night we dropped a lot of fresh mines. An E-boat must have plowed right into one of them."

The men at the ASDIC turned to the Captain to say, "All clear now. Not getting anything at all."

"Tell the MTB's to stop making smoke," the Captain said to his signalman, and the blinker began to dot-and-dash. Its light was so strong that it could even penetrate the fog. Within a few minutes the smoke stopped and we sailed out of it into the clear night air.

Twice during the night small groups of German bombers attacked us, but twice the Spitfires drove them away. The moonlight was so bright that the fighter pilots had no trouble finding the German bombers. From the bridge we saw three of them streak down in flames. The night seemed endless, but morning finally came.

It was a golden dawn, and the sun gleamed brightly on the sides of our forty little ships. The water of the Channel looked very blue that morning.

Then the Captain pointed ahead. "There's Pompey."

No Naval man ever calls Portsmouth by its real name. For a hundred years they have called it Pompey, with the accent on the first syllable.

This was our port. The beaches of Portsmouth gleamed whitely. There were several destroyers anchored off shore. The piers at the Navy Yard seemed to be crowded with people looking out toward us.

"They're counting us," the Captain said with a chuckle. "They know that forty of us left. I guess they never expected that all forty of us would arrive. It wasn't a bad trip, was it?" he asked.

"No, it wasn't," I admitted.

"I'm sorry we couldn't give you more excitement," the Captain said. "But it's getting so that the RAF is taking the excitement out of a trip through the Channel."

As we were tying up at our pier I said to the Captain, "If the Germans were smart, they'd come over right now. Here, in this harbor, they could strike forty ships laden with supplies. I wonder why they don't take a crack at them?"

The Captain laughed. "Take a look up above."

I looked up, and there, high above, circling lazily, were twelve Spitfires. The pilots were probably just hoping that the German bombers would come over!

That night I had dinner with the Captain at the Officers' Club. After dinner we turned on the radio.

"Let's see what Lord Haw-Haw has to say," the Captain said.

Lord Haw-Haw broadcast from Berlin every night in English. He began by saying, "Last night the German Air Force bombed and destroyed a convoy of forty ships that attempted to go through the English Channel and reach Portsmouth. All forty ships were destroyed."

The Captain laughed and turned off the radio.

CHAPTER 7

The Fliers at Biggin Hill

ON AUGUST 28, 1940, AFTER THE BATTLE OF Britain had been raging for twenty days, the German radio announced that the Luftwaffe was going to "ground the fighters of the Royal Air Force."

It was their plan to bomb every airport in England where the Spitfires and the Hurricanes were stationed. The Germans believed that once they had destroyed the fighter planes, it would be easy to bomb London right off the map. They knew that if they ever destroyed London they would destroy England along with it. London was the heart of England; if the heart stopped beating the country would die.

There were more than a hundred airfields in England now, and a great many of them were behind the coast of the British Channel. There were airfields at Kenley, North Weald, Hornchurch, Debden, Lympne, Detling, Northold and Biggin Hill. There were others in the north, guarding Manchester and Birmingham and Liverpool. However, right now the Germans were after London, so those I have mentioned were the most important; they were guarding the capital.

One of the best-known airfields in England was at Biggin Hill, only a few miles south of London. In the last two weeks of August the Spitfires and Hurricanes stationed at Biggin Hill had destroyed 110 German airplanes. Then one night the German radio announced that Biggin

Hill had been bombed and that every plane there had gone up in flames. I went to Biggin Hill to see if this was true.

I arrived at about eight o'clock in the morning and met the wing commander who was in charge of the airport. (In the RAF a wing commander is the same rank as a colonel in our air force.) This was Wing Commander Albert Brown, and everyone called him Brownie. Although he was only twenty years old, he had downed eighteen German planes.

He laughed when I asked him about the broadcast. "We heard the German radio too," he said. "Hop in this jeep and I'll drive you around."

He drove me to one end of the field, where there was a squadron of twelve Hurricanes. None of them showed any signs of having been destroyed. Their pilots were relaxing in a tent, listening to a portable radio.

Then Brownie took me to the other end of the field. Here there were two squadrons of Spitfires (twenty-four planes). This was the average strength of a fighter airport. Brownie suggested that we stop to watch the pilots who were playing what he called football.

"I wish you would stop calling this game football," I said to him. "It's soccer to us."

Brownie laughed. "We've called it football for about two hundred years in England, and it's too late for us to change the name now."

The pilots were all laughing happily as they kicked the ball around. There was a tent near by, and Brownie took me inside. There was a telephone in the tent.

"If that phone rings three times," Brownie said, "the boys stop playing football. That phone is connected with Air Force headquarters. As soon as the German planes start over the Channel toward England, our radar picks them up.

If the planes are coming this way, that phone rings three times."

Brownie introduced me to a young pilot, Squadron Leader Arthur Douglas. (A squadron leader would be a first lieutenant in the American Air Force.) Douglas, who was only eighteen, told me he had just graduated from high school.

"But this is a lot more fun than geometry." He laughed. Then he said shyly, "Would you like to see my airplane?"

I walked toward his Spitfire with him and he showed me how to climb into the cockpit. Then he explained the purposes of the instruments on the dashboard. I was surprised to find that the windshield was made of glass nearly three inches thick. It was bulletproof, too. At the top of the windshield there was a little mirror, like those found in automobiles.

"What's that for?" I asked Douglas. "So you can be sure your hair is combed?"

"No," and Douglas grinned. "That mirror tells us if there's a German plane on our tail. Maybe you've noticed that none of us wears a collar or tie. We spend half our time turning our necks looking to the right, looking up above, and looking to the left. That's the only way we can keep from being surprised by Jerry planes. After a scramble we usually have stiff necks."

(In the RAF the pilots never say that they had a fight. They always say they had a scramble.)

"Grab the stick with your right hand," Douglas suggested.

What he called a stick is really a small wheel about five inches across. The wheel makes the plane go up or down, and steers it, too. There is a small button on the wheel, and on this the pilot always keeps his thumb. On the instrument board there is an oblong piece of glass with a red circle on it. Two black lines cross the circle.

That is the sight for the guns. When the pilot sees an enemy plane in the circle at the point where the two lines cross, he presses the button

with his thumb and the eight guns begin to fire.

"Don't do it, though," Douglas said quickly as he saw my hand go for the wheel and my thumb reach for the button. "The safety catch isn't on."

In all, there were twenty-four clocklike instruments on the dashboard. Douglas explained them to me one by one.

"You should have been here about an hour ago," he said casually. "We had a real good scramble over the Channel and we got six Messerschmitts."

"Did you get any?" I asked him.

"I was lucky enough to get one," he said. "You know, we can always talk to one another when we're up there in a scramble. We were going along peacefully at twenty thousand feet when I heard one of my pals through my earphones. 'Hey, Doug,' he was yelling, 'you'd better look behind you. You've got a Messerschmitt on your tail.' I gave a quick look, and he was right. I did a sharp vertical climb and got away. Just then I saw the pal who had given me the warning. I also noticed two Jerry planes on his tail. I yelled to him, 'You'd better look behind yourself.' "

"Did he look behind?" I asked.

Douglas turned his face away. "Not soon enough," he said. "They got him."

The cockpit of a Spitfire is very small. I asked Douglas if he had ever had to bail out, and how he did it.

"I had to jump only three days ago," he said. "I was over the Channel when my plane got hit. The engine was on fire, and I knew that I couldn't make land. So I unfastened my belt, turned the airplane over on its back, and just fell out. That's the easiest way to bail out of a Spitfire, and I might say that the water in the Channel is very cold."

"Who picked you up?" I asked.

"One of those little motor torpedo boats that help guard the convoys in the Channel," Douglas replied. "You met Wing Commander Brown. He's a fine chap, but he's got a funny sense of humor. He had the gall to tell me I bailed out just to get a new uniform free!"

As we walked back into the tent, I noticed that it was ten o'clock. Just then the phone rang once, twice, three times. It rang very loudly, and the pilots who had been playing football stopped. Everything was suddenly quiet.

Wing Commander Brown picked up the receiver. "Yes, sir," he said. "Twenty-four plus off Folkestone at thirty thousand feet. Righto."

Squadron Leader Douglas left the tent and cried out, "A scramble, twenty-four plus off Folkestone. Let's get going."

They all ran for their planes, and within a few seconds the engines were roaring. Brownie explained to me that "twenty-four plus off Folkestone" meant that at least twenty-four German planes had been sighted over the Channel. They were approaching the city of Folkestone, which was only about thirty miles from Biggin Hill.

Brownie picked up a small "walkie-talkie" from the table and walked outside with it. When he spoke into it his voice could be heard all over the field.

"Red flight take off," he cried, and three of the Spitfires wheeled around, taxied to the runway, and then streaked off. Next Brownie ordered Yellow flight to take off, then Blue flight, and finally Green flight.

"Douglas is the leader of this squadron," Brownie explained to me. "When he gets up there he's the boss. By the time his squadron intercepts the German planes, they may have split up. Then Douglas will say, 'Yellow flight turn north, Blue flight turn south.' That's why we split a squadron of twelve planes up into four flights."

"How soon will they be back?" I asked, as the Spitfires disappeared into the distance.

"I never worry about how soon they will be back," Brownie said quietly, "but I always worry about *how many* will get back."

"Hard to believe they're up there now fighting German planes," I said. "Tell me what the Luftwaffe planes are like."

"They're good," he said thoughtfully. "Not as good as our Spitfires, but they're good. The ME-109 has a single cannon that fires right through the propeller. It has four machine guns in its wings and two more which, like the cannon, fire through the revolving blades of the propeller. They can hit you from eight hundred yards away," he said grimly.

"What about their two-engined Messerschmitt?" I asked.

"That's the ME-110," he said. "It has two cannon and four machine guns. Then they have the Heinkel-113, which we just love to see. It's real fast—does three hundred and eighty miles an hour—but it has only one cannon and two machine guns. And when you hit a Heinkel it goes down." Then Brownie asked, "Do you know the hardest part of being a Commanding Officer?"

I shook my head.

"The waiting," he said. "Waiting for the boys to come back."

CHAPTER 8

The RAF in Action

THE TIME PASSED VERY SLOWLY AS WE WAITED for them to return. In the quiet and peaceful countryside it was hard to believe that twelve young pilots who a few minutes ago had been playing football were now probably fighting for their lives.

Brownie and I walked over to the headquarters building. Everyone was sitting around, just waiting. Then finally we heard the faint sound of engines. We walked outside and far above we could see a group of planes coming toward us.

"Are they ours?" I asked Brownie.

"Yes," and he laughed. "If they were German planes we would have been warned. You know, no matter what you hear on the radio, so far the Germans haven't dropped one bomb on our airfield."

The planes came closer, and then they pealed off and "buzzed" the field. (In other words, they streaked over the field very low, dipping their wings from side to side.) The roar of the engines was deafening. One plane after another swooped down.

"That's good news," and Brownie laughed again. "They only buzz the field when the mission has been successful, and I hope you noticed that all twelve airplanes came back."

Then the Spitfires landed, one by one. Each pilot had to report exactly what had happened. When all the reports were in, Wing Commander Brown would have a good idea of the damage inflicted upon the enemy. He would then relay this information to Air Force headquarters in London. Because he was the Squadron Leader, Arthur Douglas reported first.

"We met them just over Folkestone at twenty thousand feet," he said. "There were about fifteen bombers, and above them twelve Messerschmitts. Luckily, the sun was in back of us and we were able to get fairly close before they spotted us. I sent a four-second burst at a Heinkel. It plunged toward the Channel, smoke pouring out of it."

"Did any of you others notice that?"

"I did," one of the pilots said. "In fact, I followed that Heinkel right down to the deck. You can never call that one a probable."

(Before a pilot got credit for downing a German plane, someone else had to vouch for having seen the plane crash. Then it was called "confirmed." If a pilot stated that he downed a

German plane but none of the rest of the squadron noticed it, it was listed as unconfirmed or as a "probable.")

"Okay, Douglas, go on."

"I told Blue flight and Yellow flight to 'angel' up to twenty-five thousand feet while the rest of us kept the Jerries busy," Douglas went on. "A Messerschmitt got on my tail and I banked away and hid in a cloud. I regrouped my flight and we went after the bombers, which were then heading toward London. At a hundred yards I sent a three-second burst into one of the Heinkels. It exploded in flames. Just then Blue and Yellow flights attacked the Heinkels, and I'm sure they got at least six of them. But I was too busy fighting off those Messerschmitts to get a good count."

One by one the pilots reported. The reports were immediately typed up and one checked against the other.

Then Wing Commander Brown said to me, smiling, "I make it nine confirmed enemy planes and four probables. Not a bad hour's work. I doubt if any of those bombers reached London. Those that got away from us were picked up by fighters from another airport."

We walked out onto the field. I noticed that two mechanics were standing with Douglas beside his plane. I walked over to see what they were doing.

"Look at this," Douglas said, pointing angrily. In the fuselage of the Spitfire, there was a hole you could stick your fist through.

"I never even knew they hit me," Douglas said, very annoyed that his plane had been damaged.

The mechanics worked fast. They glued heavy airplane cloth over the hole. After they had dabbed on some paint, it was impossible to tell that the plane had ever been hit.

Gasoline trucks were hurrying from one plane to another, filling up their tanks, and crew men were replacing ammunition in the guns.

"You won't have to go up again today, will you?" I asked Douglas.

He shrugged his shoulders. "As you see, we have three squadrons here. We take turns going up. But sometimes the Germans send over so many planes that we all go up at once."

At that moment we heard three loud rings from the telephone. Then everything was quiet until the Wing Commander came out of the tent.

"A scramble," he cried, just as he had done before. "Looks like a big show. All squadrons take off. Forty-eight plus approaching Dover at twenty-five thousand feet."

Douglas grabbed his parachute and slipped into the straps. Then I gave him a boost onto the

wing of his plane. He climbed into the cockpit and started his engine.

"Good luck, kid," I shouted at him.

"I might need it," he yelled back, grinning.

I guess he needed more luck than I had to give him. Fifteen minutes later he was dead.

CHAPTER 9

The Eagle Squadron

IT WAS GLOOMY AT BIGGIN HILL THAT NIGHT. Everyone was thinking of poor Douglas. Wing Commander Brown gave the boys a little talk after dinner.

"Douglas was our pal," he said simply, "but we can't afford to brood about what happened to him. We'll all miss him, but let's not allow this to get us down. Douglas died for his country. There's no better way to die than that. And he died fighting in his aircraft. That's the way he wanted to die. He belonged to Squadron A, and

73

I know how you men feel. I've arranged for the Squadron to have a week's leave. You will leave tonight."

They cheered up a bit at that. They could go home and be with their families for a week. A little later cars came and drove them to London, only forty miles away. Everyone who was left behind went to bed early that night.

At Biggin Hill and at the other fighter airfields the day began at sunrise, which was about 5:00 A.M. Just before breakfast we heard the sound of planes coming toward the field.

"Come outside," Wing Commander Brown suggested to me. Then he smiled. "There are some lads you'll want to meet. Squadron A is being replaced by the Yanks."

Twelve Spitfires circled the field, landed, and then taxied up to the headquarters building. The pilots hopped out and reported to the Wing Commander. They were all members of the fa-

Red Tobin

mous Eagle Squadron—American boys who felt
that sooner or later we'd be in the war, and why
wait?

They all wore the regular RAF uniforms, but
they didn't wear the regular RAF English accents. It was fun to hear a lot of American voices.
The RAF pilots treated the boys like conquering

heroes. To them these Americans were something really special. Their country wasn't even in the war, and yet here they were fighting for democracy.

They received the regular RAF pilot's pay, which was the equivalent of only about sixteen dollars a week. That wasn't so bad for the English pilots. When they received a leave they could go home and stay with their parents. When the Eagle Squadron boys were given a leave, there was no place for them to go but to London, where prices were very high.

There was one tall, red-headed American boy I took to right away. His name was Gene Tobin (they called him "Red"), and up to six months before he had been working in Hollywood. His job had been to guide visitors through one of the big movie studios. On week ends he used to take flying lessons, and he had learned to fly the little Piper Cub.

"About six months ago," Gene Tobin told me earnestly, "I got real mad at the way the Germans were pushing everybody around. I knew that sooner or later they'd start to push us around too, and we'd be in the war. So, when I heard that some other Americans felt as I did and that they were forming an American squadron, I joined up."

"And you've only had six months' training?" I asked. Usually a fighter pilot had at least a year's training before they gave him a Spitfire.

"That's all." Gene Tobin grinned. "I had to tell them a few white lies. I told them that I had flown fighter planes at home. So they gave me a Spitfire right away. Boy, I'll never forget my first flight!"

"Is the Spitfire hard to fly, Gene?" I asked him.

"Not if you're used to it," and he grinned again. "But the Piper Cubs I'd flown made only a hundred and twenty-five miles an hour. These

Spitfires go more than three hundred miles an hour. Just before I went up in the Spitfire an English pilot said to me, 'Never let the airplane get in front of you.' "

"What did he mean by that?" I asked.

"He meant simply that if you try to make a quick turn at that speed, you'll black right out," Gene explained. "When you fly an ordinary plane you can afford to make mistakes. But you can't afford to make mistakes in a Spitfire going at three hundred miles an hour."

"How do you like being in the RAF?" I asked.

"Great," Gene said. "I never knew any English people before. Don't let their accents fool you. They're the toughest guys I ever met. Another thing I like about the RAF is that we have eggs for breakfast every morning."

An hour later the telephone rang three times, and Red Tobin, Gus Daymond, Gordon Peterson (a Mormon from Utah), and Jimmy Crowley all whooped with delight and ran to their planes. I stood with Wing Commander Brown as they took off. He watched them very carefully.

"Those boys aren't fooling me," he said. "I know that a number of them lied to get into the RAF. They all said they'd had a lot of flying experience. But they're learning, all right. They took off nicely. I told the C-Squadron to cover them until they get a little more practice."

"What do you mean by 'covering' them?" I asked Brownie.

"Protect them," he explained. "C-Squadron is an experienced bunch. I told them to stay three thousand feet above the Eagle boys to keep the Germans from diving on them. In another week that won't be necessary."

The Eagle boys went up three times that day. The third time they came back wagging their wings. When they landed they all rushed to Gus Daymond and Gordon Peterson, threw their arms around them, and slapped them on the backs. Both Gus and Pete had downed German bombers. It wasn't long before these two were recognized as two of the best fighter pilots in the whole RAF.

That night the pilots all sat around the Biggin Hill mess—big Oscar Coen, Bill Geiger, Jack Festler, Andy Mamedoff, Bill Hall, Danny Daniels—and I got to know them.

One of the Eagle Squadron boys played the piano and the others sang American college songs. They sang the Maine Stein Song and the Whiffenpoof Song. The English pilots loved the tunes, and then they sang their special RAF songs. When they found out that Red Tobin was from Hollywood, they all started asking him questions about movie stars. To hear Red tell it, he knew every star in Hollywood. He told some wonderful stories about them.

At ten o'clock it was lights out, and everyone

went to bed. Red Tobin whispered to me, "Don't let on, but I never met a movie star in my life—but how could I disappoint these guys? If you come from Hollywood they all think that you have to know Clark Gable and Cary Grant. I couldn't disappoint them, could I?"

"No, you couldn't, Red," I said solemnly.

CHAPTER 10

I Fly in an RAF Intruder

WING COMMANDER BROWN TOLD ME ABOUT something new that the RAF pilots were doing.

"The German bombers are coming over a great deal at night, as you know," he said. "You also know about our ordinary night fighters. But now we have something new—night fighters who are called 'Intruders.' These Intruders fly an American airplane, the two-motored Douglas Boston. You Yanks call it the A-20A. These Intruders don't go up to intercept the German bombers as they aim toward London or other English cities."

82

Squadron Leader Richard Hooper

"Where do they go?" I asked.

"They fly over France and Holland and Germany, looking for enemy airports. When they locate a German airport they keep flying over it, waiting for the German bombers to return after bombing England. The German bombers never expect to find RAF fighter planes over their own airports. Our boys have knocked down a lot of them during the past few weeks."

"But don't the ground crews at the German airports recognize the RAF planes flying up there?" I asked.

Wing Commander Brown laughed. "No, they don't. When the German planes return from a mission, they all use landing lights of the same color. They use either white, red, or green lights. To help us, the French underground finds out what color the German planes will use each night. The French have radios hidden in cellars, and they radio this information to RAF headquarters. When the Intruders fly over the German airports, they always have landing lights of the right color. So the ground crews, naturally, think they are German airplanes."

As I laughed, Brownie said casually, "How

would you like to take a flight with one of our Intruder squadrons?"

"I'd love to," I replied.

There was an Intruder squadron at an airdrome about forty miles away from Biggin Hill. Brownie drove me there, and introduced me to the commanding officer, Squadron Leader Richard Hooper. Hooper was a tall, lanky pilot who was only twenty-one. He had laughing eyes and a long, blond handlebar mustache of which he was very proud.

"I've got the longest mustache in the whole RAF," he boasted. "As you know, the fighter pilots in the RAF always leave the top button of their coats unbuttoned. You can always tell a fighter pilot that way. The bomber pilots always keep that top button buttoned. We wanted to do something to show that we were Intruders, so we all grew long mustaches. Want to take a little trip with me tonight?" he asked.

"Sure," I said. "You just tell me what to do."

"Well, we sleep all day and fly all night. I'll show you your room, and maybe you can take a nap."

The pilots at this airdrome lived in a lovely old red brick house, which before the war had been a girls' school. Because the pilots slept during the daytime, all the windows had been painted black to keep the rooms dark. I slept awhile, and then Squadron Leader Hooper woke me. After dinner, he took me out to see his airplane.

"You ought to know this airplane," he said. "It was made in your country, out in California. We carry a crew of three—the pilot, the rear gunner, and the observer. Tonight you'll be the observer. Here's where you sit."

He pointed out a glass-enclosed place in the nose of the airplane. He fitted a parachute on me, and I squeezed into the glass compartment.

It was a tight squeeze. Hooper motioned to me to put on a pair of earphones that were hanging there. Meanwhile, he climbed up to the pilot's cockpit just above me. When he talked I could hear him plainly through the earphones. Then he started the two motors.

It was hot there in the glass nose, and I could hardly move because of the heavy parachute harness. I knew I'd never have nerve enough to jump anyhow, so I slipped out of the harness and felt more comfortable.

Squadron Leader Hooper called, "Everything all right?"

"Everything lovely," I told him.

"We'll take a trip over the English Channel," he said. "You can talk to me any time you wish. There's an airport outside of Paris we might look over. Here we go."

We rushed down the black concrete runway, and then we were in the air. We rose sharply, circled once and headed for the Channel, only a few miles away.

The moon hanging high over the Channel was an orange ball. Now and then swirling white wisps of cloud flew in front of us. We were flying low, and I could see that the Channel was very smooth. I felt quite alone up there, and I hoped that the glass was strong.

"Any chance of my falling through this glass?" I yelled.

Hooper heard me through his earphones. "That glass is so strong you can't even kick a hole in it," he assured me.

"How fast are we going?" I asked.

"Exactly three hundred and ten miles an hour," he said calmly. "Look ahead. There's France."

I looked ahead, and there were the jagged cliffs of the French coast, ghostly in the yellow moonlight.

We flew very low to make it impossible for the German radio stations to pick us up on their radar. When we reached the French coast we climbed up to about three thousand feet. France was completely blacked out.

"In case you're wondering why they aren't shooting at us," Squadron Leader Hooper said, "they never shoot at a single airplane. That's why we don't travel in company. . . . See that little river below us? That's the Somme."

"Take a look to the left," I heard through my earphones a moment later. I looked, and about five miles away there was a wonderful display of fireworks. Red and white streaks were shooting into the sky. It was like Coney Island on the Fourth of July.

"That's Calais," the pilot announced through the intercommunication.

"Let's get closer," I yelled.

"Not a chance." The pilot laughed. "Those

lights look pretty, but they're very nasty anti-aircraft shells. We're as close to Calais as I want to get."

Then we headed for Paris.

CHAPTER 11

Rescue of a Pilot at Sea

THERE WERE BARRAGE BALLOONS OVER PARIS, so we climbed to 5,000 feet.

"I'm going to put our lights on now," Hooper called. "I hope we've got the right color."

A few seconds later I saw green lights blinking at the tip of each wing. If the Germans were using green lights tonight, we were all right.

Paris gleamed brightly in the moonlight. The RAF never bombed Paris. There were no factories there, and the RAF didn't want to take the chance of hitting the Louvre, the Eiffel Tower, or any of the other buildings and monuments which have made Paris the most beautiful city in the world. Even though Paris was blacked out, it gleamed in the white light of the moon. Looking down, I could see the Eiffel Tower and the broad street called the Champs Elysées. And then we were across the city, and Hooper began to circle.

"That is Le Bourget, the Paris airport," he said.

We continued to circle for about fifteen minutes, and I knew he was hoping that some German bombers would return to land there. But it looked as though ours was the only plane in the air.

"Getting a little low on gas," Hooper called to me. "I think we'll go down, drop our eggs on those hangars, and go home. Hang on."

I hung on, and as he swooped downward, the

ground seemed to rush up at us. I could see the whole airfield through the "goldfish bowl" I was sitting in. It looked as though we were going to dive right into the ground. Then the nose of the plane came up sharply and I felt a little lurch.

"There go our eggs," Hooper called to me.

A second later I heard six quick explosions and, looking back, I could see the bombs we had dropped raising quick, bright flashes. Then a burst of fire appeared. Hooper had hit a hangar, all right, and the hangar must have had a lot of gasoline stored in it.

Hooper wasn't waiting around to see what damage we had done. Our plane was streaking toward the Channel now. We crossed the French coast and then we were over the Channel, flying only about four hundred feet above the water. The two engines made a beautiful sound. It was as though they were singing, "Don't worry, don't worry, we'll get you home."

"Are there any lighthouses in the Channel?"
I called through the intercom.

"No lighthouses out here," the pilot answered.

I was sure I had seen a light flashing down
there in the water. I looked below again, and
then I was sure of it. The light fluttered irregu-
larly, like the heartbeat of a tired bird.

"It may not be a lighthouse," I said, "but
somebody down there is flashing a light."

Hooper heard me, and as he banked the plane
to the right I could see the light distinctly.

"It *is* a light," I heard through my earphones,
and his voice sounded excited. "It's flashing—
golly, it's flashing SOS."

We circled low, and every now and then we'd
see the light flashing, three short lights, three
long lights, three short lights, which is SOS in
any language. Then I heard the pilot talking,
but he wasn't talking to me.

"Calling angel, calling angel," he said, and

his voice wasn't gay and laughing now. "Angel" was the code name for the airfield we had left about two hours before.

"Are you receiving?" Hooper went on. "Over."

Another voice broke in. "Angel receiving you clearly. Over."

My pilot called back, "Take my position fix."

He stopped, and a moment later the voice said, "Have your position exactly. Are you returning now? Why do you wish position fix? Over."

Then Hooper said, "Receiving SOS from Channel right below us. Probably fighter pilot who bailed out."

From the airport came the voice, "Will contact rescue ships at Brighton immediately. We have the exact position, so return."

"Okay," Hooper said calmly.

We stopped circling and headed for home.

"They have a lot of fast rescue launches at Brighton," Hooper told me through the intercom. "Those things go about forty-five miles an hour, and that fellow down there is only fifteen miles from Brighton. The rescue boats will be there in no time."

Ten minutes later we were circling over our airfield. Below there was a thin triangle of lights.

"That's home," said Squadron Leader Hooper with a chuckle. "When there are any Germans about, they don't show any lights at all down there. Then we have to feel our way in."

He landed the plane gently, and we taxied up to the Operations building. As we entered the brightly lighted office, we heard the radio crackling. Then, when the radio operator tuned it to the proper wave length, a voice called, "This is Brighton, Motor Rescue Squad. Just picked up fighter pilot Jack Edgerton from Channel. He wishes to thank Intruder pilot who spotted him."

Hooper laughed and said to me, "Funny job we have in the RAF—every night we go over there, bombing German airdromes or shooting down German bombers. We do it so often it gets to be routine. There's nothing exciting about it. But it *is* exciting to spot some pilot down there in the Channel and know that because you spotted him he was saved."

CHAPTER 12

London in the Blackout

WE WENT INTO THE OPERATIONS ROOM SO HOOPER could report what he had done. You could sit there and know what was happening all over England. Liverpool, far to the north, was being bombed that night. The Germans hadn't bombed London yet, but it was only midnight.

"You spend most of your time in London, don't you?" Hooper asked me.

When I told him I did, he said, "How would you like to see how London looks from the air at night?"

By now I had such confidence in this lanky pilot with the funny-looking mustache that I would have gone anywhere with him. I climbed into the glass nose of his plane, and once again we skimmed along the runway.

Some pilots are "ham-handed." That means they have a heavy touch on the controls of a plane. Ham-handed pilots jerk a plane into the air. Hooper wasn't like that at all. It was as though he and the airplane were one and he could "think" it off the runway. When he pulled the stick back, the plane rose gradually and gracefully. You felt that this was a good, honest airplane, as trustworthy as were the men in the Douglas factory in California who had built it. The plane climbed up into the night.

"We're at five thousand feet now," Hooper called to me. "Isn't this airplane a sweetheart?"

"It was made in America," I told him, and then I added, "but you know how to fly her, all right."

Suddenly there was London, sprawling below us. Not a sign of light was to be seen in the city. London was really blacked out. But I knew that London had a thousand eyes; I knew that those mechanical radar eyes were on us now. They knew that we were a friendly airplane. Although London seemed still and lifeless, I was aware that there were anti-aircraft crews all over the city, plotting our course.

Then below us was the lovely Thames River,

looking like a silver ribbon. The moon was so bright that I could count the six bridges across the Thames.

Then I saw the huge dome of St. Paul's Cathedral, guarding the city as it had guarded it for two hundred years. Far below I could see Fleet Street, where all the London newspapers had offices. Many of my pals were down there, getting out the next morning's papers.

London looked asleep, but I knew that there were 30,000 firemen, ambulance drivers, and air wardens wide awake just in case the Germans came over. London was asleep, but in her sleep she was well guarded.

In the east a very thin ribbon of light showed, and my pilot called, "Time we had breakfast, chum." We circled away from London and headed for our airport.

Our plane was like a horse hurrying home to

the barn for its oats. We streaked through the night, and then we landed lightly on the concrete runway.

Inside the mess hall, we found about thirty pilots having an early breakfast. They were all telling of what they had done that night. One pilot had shot down three German bombers as they approached their airdrome in Holland. Others had started fires on enemy airfields. All of them had great praise for their American airplane, which they called the Boston.

The pilots sat around for an hour or so "talking shop." The Battle of Britain had been going on for over two months now, and they all felt that the tide was beginning to turn.

"As soon as the Germans realized they couldn't bomb England by daylight without suffering terrible losses, they were licked," Squadron Leader Hooper said. "Ever since the Spitfires destroyed so many of them during those daylight raids, the German pilots have been deathly afraid of the Spitfires."

"How do you know they're so afraid of the Spitfires?" I asked.

"Well, I'll tell you," he said with a twinkle in his eye. "The other day I went to Tunbridge Wells to visit a pal of mine who's in the hospital there. At this hospital they had some wounded German pilots. In fact, they had twelve of them. I thought it would be fun to take a look at them, so I went into their ward with a doctor. He went from one to another, and then he yelled angrily to the nurse who was in charge, 'Every one of these German pilots is covered with black-and-blue marks. How did they get all those bruises?'"

" 'It isn't our fault, Doctor,' the nurse said calmly. 'One of these German pilots was delirious all last night. He kept yelling, "Spitfire,

Spitfire." And every time he yelled "Spitfire," why those eleven other Germans just naturally bailed out of bed!' "

The pilots all roared with laughter at Hooper's story.

I said, "Hooper, tonight I learned two things about you. First, I learned that you are a great pilot, and now I learn that you're a great liar."

He grinned and said, "Well, I have had lots of practice at both."

CHAPTER 13

The RAF Takes the Offensive

FOR A SOLID MONTH THE GERMAN AIR FORCE
attacked England every day. It bombed London
and set fire to the city at least twenty times. But
at the end of that period London was still standing. German planes had bombed Coventry and
Liverpool and Plymouth and a great many other
cities, and had hurt them. But every time the
enemy bombers came over in daylight, the RAF
fighters destroyed dozens of them.

When a German bomber was shot down, Germany lost not only a plane but also a trained crew

105

Flag of the Royal Air Force

of five men. The planes could be replaced, but it was hard to replace the pilots, the navigators, the radio operators, and the bombardiers. The enemy had learned that he could neither stop the convoys going through the Channel nor destroy London by daylight bombing. As a result, the Germans decided to start night bombing.

It was now late September, 1940, and at last the RAF was ordered to take the offensive. The bomber pilots received orders to cross the Channel and to bomb airfields and war plants which were operating in Germany, France and Holland. French and Dutch resistance fighters were sneaking across the Channel to give the RAF the exact locations of these important airfields and factories.

Every day now supplies were coming from America. President Roosevelt had said, "We will give England all help—short of war," and Winston Churchill had told him, "Give us the tools and we will finish the job."

Every day more of these "tools" came to British ports. Fast little P-40's, fighter planes which the RAF called The Tomahawks, and little P-37's, which were called The Mohawks, arrived. So did a lot of medium bombers, which the British called The Hudsons. American factories in Los Angeles, Detroit, and Seattle were helping England to fight back.

A month before, the German Air Force had outnumbered the RAF about ten to one. But a thousand German planes had been destroyed by the RAF and the anti-aircraft guns. Meanwhile the RAF had grown. The odds were now only about two to one, and, although the odds were still in favor of Germany, Churchill gave the order to strike back. England was tired of taking it—now she would give Germany some of her own medicine. She would carry the Battle of Britain to enemy shores.

I went to a base about a hundred miles from London to see how the bombers operated. The English bombers were big Whitleys and Lancasters. Wing Commander James Kenney was in charge of the field. The pilots all called him the "Old Man," a name they always gave to commanding officers. Kenney wasn't really very old. He was only twenty-three!

I arrived at the airfield late in the afternoon,

and the ground crews were "bombing up" the planes. "Old Man" Kenney showed me his big bomber. The five-hundred-pound bombs had just been hoisted up into the bomb bays. The bombs were painted bright yellow, and they looked very innocent.

"In about six hours I'm going to drop these on Hamburg," Kenney said. "Do you want to send a message to anyone in Germany?"

"Sure," I told him, and I took out a pencil and wrote on the bright yellow side of one of the bombs, "Love and kisses." Under that I signed my name.

Kenney was just as proud of his big Whitley as the fighter pilots were of their little Spitfires. He told me that if I would climb up into the plane, he'd explain the different parts to me. We went into the cockpit. It was a cozy little nest. Kenney sat in the pilot's seat and tried to explain how some of the instruments worked, but it was all much too complicated for me to understand. In the little cockpit there was room for a co-pilot, the bombardier, and the navigator.

"The navigator is the most important man in our crew," Kenney said. "I only fly the airplane, but I never quite know where we are. No matter how dark it is, your navigator does know."

As we walked back through the fuselage of the big bomber, I noticed a pile of neatly stacked flares. These would be dropped over Hamburg, and would light up the whole city. I saw parachutes, too, and extra ammunition. In the very rear of the bomber was the gun turret. It had four guns that shot four thousand rounds a minute. The turret revolved so that the bombardier could sight a German plane if it was above him or on either side of him.

We climbed down from the plane and Kenney looked at his watch. It was time to give final instructions. We walked past the eleven other planes that were to take part in that night's raid. Then we entered a building on which there was a sign reading, "Operations."

Upstairs we walked into a large room that looked like a high-school classroom. Beside a blackboard which hung on the front wall, there was a huge map of Germany. This room was called the "briefing room." About sixty pilots, bombardiers, and navigators were waiting there for Kenney. When he arrived, they quieted down to listen to their instructions.

"This is our target for tonight," Kenney said, pointing to Hamburg on the big map. "The weather should be good all the way. You should be over Hamburg exactly at midnight. Be sure to stay away from the residential part of the city. Our job is to bomb the targets to the north of Hamburg. As soon as you drop your bombs, radio back here to headquarters. Any questions?"

One pilot held up a hand. "We haven't been

over Hamburg before," he said. "How good is their anti-aircraft fire?"

"Very good," Kenney said solemnly. "Stay above twenty thousand feet. You have a full moon tonight, and should be able to find the factories easily. It will be daylight at 5:30 A.M., so once you drop your bombs come home fast. We don't want to be caught over Germany in daylight."

There were no more questions and, like boys in any classroom, the airmen piled out of the door, laughing. Then they headed for the mess, where the tables were laden with bread, butter, cakes, and big pots of tea.

It was growing dark outside and nearing time for the take-off. But the men still laughed and joked. No one would have guessed that they were going on one of the most dangerous trips ever made. Finally they left the mess hall. Each man grabbed his parachute, his heavy flying coat, and his warm boots. Then they got into jeeps which took them out to where their twelve planes were being warmed up by mechanics.

I walked with Kenney to his plane. "Wish you were coming along," he said cheerfully. "Looks like a nice night."

Then he climbed up the tiny ladder into the big bomber. His crew followed him.

The noise of the twelve planes was terrific as pilots warmed up their engines. The planes looked like big dozing beetles. One wondered how they could ever get off the ground.

Then they began to move, Kenney's plane first in line. As they roared down the runway they didn't look big and clumsy any more. One by one they lifted themselves into the air. They circled once and then headed for Hamburg.

The airdrome seemed strangely quiet now, and lonely as a college campus looks and feels at vacation time. I walked back to the mess, and

Wing Commander Rod Farmer, who was the commanding officer when Kenney was flying, asked me if I wanted to see the Operations Room.

It was completely dark now, but the Operations Room was brightly lighted. This was the heart of the airfield. Here there were radios and telephones and maps, and here Wing Commander Farmer could follow the movements of Kenney's squadron.

"We won't hear from the boys until just before they reach Hamburg," he said. "They keep radio silence until then so the German night fighters can't locate them."

We sat there quietly—the wing commander, the radio operators, and I. I kept thinking of tall, smiling, good-looking Jim Kenney and his crew, who even now were flying over Germany. Then suddenly there was a crackling from the radio.

"Approaching target," a calm voice said.

"That," Wing Commander Farmer said, "was Jim Kenney."

CHAPTER 14

Another Mission Accomplished

IN THE CENTER OF THE OPERATIONS ROOM THERE was a big table, and on it lay a very large map. As the planes reported "Approaching target," Wing Commander Farmer put little toy planes on the map. When all twelve planes had reported, there were twelve little toy planes at the place marked Hamburg.

"As soon as the pilots drop their bombs and start home, they'll report again," Farmer said. "Right now they're too busy to talk to us. They're making their run for their targets, and they're trying to duck the anti-aircraft fire."

"Is the flak always heavy over Hamburg?" I asked. (The RAF boys always called anti-aircraft fire flak.)

"I was over there a week ago," the Wing Commander said solemnly, "and I promise you, the flak was so heavy you could get out and walk on it."

I could imagine what it was like over Hamburg—a hundred long white fingers of light reaching into the sky, trying to spot Kenney and the others. I could imagine a thousand bright, angry flashes as the anti-aircraft shells exploded.

The radio started crackling again.

"Squadron Leader Owen reporting. Okay."

Three other pilots checked in, just using their names and the one word, "Okay." One by one they reported, eleven of them, and then there was silence.

"What about Kenney?" I asked Wing Commander Farmer. "We haven't heard from him yet."

"No, we haven't," he said quietly.

He moved eleven of the little toy planes away from where Hamburg was marked on the map, and pointed them in the direction of England. He left one plane, representing Kenney, at Hamburg.

"Try to raise Wing Commander Kenney," Farmer said to the radio operator.

"Arsenal calling Wing Commander Kenney. Arsenal calling Wing Commander Kenney." The radio operator repeated it over and over. Arsenal was the code name for that particular airfield. The radio operator kept on calling for fifteen minutes, but there was no answer.

It was then 2:00 A.M., and the Wing Commander moved the eleven little planes close to the German coast on the map. There was still no word from Kenney. One by one the other eleven

pilots checked in. Their voices sounded cheerful as they came through the radio. No one in the Operations Room mentioned Kenney now, but everyone was thinking of him.

"Let's go outside," Wing Commander Farmer said quietly.

We walked out of the building. It was 5:15 A.M. and the dawn was chasing the night away. Then the sun appeared over the horizon. There wasn't a cloud in the sky.

"Jim Kenney and I have been friends for a long while," Wing Commander Farmer said. "We were kids together, went to high school together, and then went to Oxford. We were in the same class. We had just finished our third year when war came, and we joined up together."

"Maybe he and his crew bailed out," I said hopefully.

Wing Commander Farmer shrugged his shoulders—and then lifted his head. Very faintly we could hear the sound of motors. And then in a few seconds the faint sound became a roar as the first bomber back came into view. It circled the field once and landed. It lumbered to its assigned spot and a jeep hurried over to pick up the crew.

Other planes arrived. The chickens were coming home to roost—but not Jim Kenney. The jeeps hurried the crews straight to the Operations Room where they would report everything that had happened.

It was bright daylight now, and the sun was warm. Eleven planes had landed and all eleven crews had gone into the building called "Operations." Wing Commander Farmer looked grave.

"Don't give up hope," he said quietly. "We never do."

And then we heard the sound of an engine— but it was so faint and far away that it might have been an automobile engine. It didn't sound very smooth. The engine backfired several times, but the sound did grow louder.

Wing Commander Farmer grabbed my arm, pointed to the south and said, "Look."

Far in the distance I could see an airplane heading toward the field. As it approached closer, the engines still sputtering, it look lopsided, and I realized that one of its wings was shorter than the other. Wing Commander Farmer barked out a couple of quick orders. A fire truck and an ambulance had been standing by. They roared out onto the field and parked at the end of the runway where the plane would land.

"That's Jimmy Kenney all right," the wing commander said grimly, "and he's in trouble. His right wing is half shot away."

The plane circled the field once, then circled it again.

"His radio must have been shot away," the wing commander said, "and his landing gear must have jammed. He circled to let us know he was in trouble and to have the fire truck and the ambulance ready. He should have his wheels down by now. Come on, let's get out there."

He hopped into a jeep and I climbed in beside him. All of the other crews had rushed out of the Operations building and were silently looking up at the injured plane. You just knew a lot of them were praying that Jimmy would be able to make a safe landing.

We went down to the edge of the runway. The ambulance was on one side of it and the fire truck on the other. The plane stopped circling, straightened out and aimed for the runway. Gradually it lost altitude. Wing Commander Farmer was thinking aloud:

"That's right, Jimmy. Ease her in. Careful, Jimmy, you've got no wheels. You've got to land it light on its belly, Jimmy. Easy, easy . . . lift the nose a bit, Jimmy, lift the nose . . . that's it. . . . Now, Jimmy, now."

It was as though Jimmy Kenney had heard him. Just as the wing commander said, "Now, Jimmy, now," the plane touched the runway.

There was a screeching noise as the belly of the plane slithered along the concrete runway. The fire truck shot right along to one side of it, and the ambulance to the other. Then the big plane swerved to the right, leaned over on its right side and came to a stop.

"Thanks, God," the wing commander said softly. "That's the greatest landing I ever saw."

The fire truck was right beside it now, but there was no need for it. A ladder was raised up to the cockpit, and we saw the grinning face of Jimmy Kenney. He climbed out and then came down the ladder, followed by the four other members of his crew.

"Sorry to be so late, Rod," Jimmy Kenney said, still grinning, "but they delayed us a little."

CHAPTER 15

Report of a Flight

TWO DOCTORS IN WHITE COATS CAME RUNNING from the ambulance.

"Anybody hurt?" they asked Kenney.

"Take care of Sergeant Hannah," he said. "He's been playing with fireworks and burned his fingers."

Sergeant Hannah was a grinning, blond-haired, eighteen-year-old rear gunner. He held out his hands. They were fiery red, and the sleeves of his flying coat looked as though they too had been burned.

Sergeant John Hannah

"Into the ambulance with you, Sergeant," one of the doctors said cheerfully. "We'll have you as good as new in no time."

The rest of us climbed into jeeps and headed back to the Operations building. All of the pilots and crews gathered around Jimmy and his men. A few minutes before they had been worried, but now that Jimmy and the crew were safe, the other fliers started to joke with them about cracking up an expensive airplane.

When we got inside, Jimmy Kenney told his story. "It was an easy flight to the target," he said. "We made our bomb run at twenty thousand feet. The weather was perfect. I never saw so much flak in my life. That stuff was bursting all around us, but we stayed on course, located our target, and then it was 'bombs away.' "

"Did you hit your target?" Wing Commander Farmer wanted to know.

"Brother, did we hit that target!" Jimmy laughed. "The factory must have been loaded with oil or gasoline. When our bombs landed, flames shot up two thousand feet high."

"How many feet?" Wing Commander Farmer asked sternly.

"Well, anyhow, five hundred feet," Jimmy said, undaunted. "And then we started for home. I was just about to radio you when we got hit. An anti-aircraft shell chewed off part of our right wing and we started to wobble all over the sky. As if that wasn't enough, a night fighter appeared from nowhere and gave us a burst. One of his shells hit our radio and put it out of commission. That's why I couldn't signal you."

"How did Sergeant Hannah get burned?" Farmer asked.

"I'll tell you how Sergeant John Hannah got burned," Jimmy said gravely. "I thought we had gotten away from the night fighter. I dived down and headed for the coast. It was hard to keep the plane on an even keel because of my battered wing. But we were doing all right until that night fighter came back. He came at us, and I heard Sergeant Hannah firing his machine guns there in the rear turret. Then I heard two explosions, one a small one inside the plane and the other a real big one."

"What was the big one?" Farmer asked.

"That was the night fighter," Jimmy answered. "Sergeant Hannah scored a direct hit on it and it exploded. The little explosion was more serious. We had been hit by an incendiary shell, and a small fire started in the fuselage. Sergeant Hannah ran from his turret and started to beat out the flames.

"If the flames had reached those flares or the extra ammunition we carried, we'd have all been dead, but Sergeant Hannah grabbed the flares and threw them overboard. He managed to move the heavy boxes of ammunition away from the flames, too. By that time the gloves were burned right off his hands. He threw his body right into the flames, rolled over and over, beating at them with his bare hands, and finally put them out."

Just then one of the doctors came in to tell Kenney that Hannah would be all right.

"His arms are burned right up to the elbows," the doctor said, "but we eased his pain and covered his burns with salve. He'll be flying again within a week."

"I'd like to recommend him for a decoration," Jimmy said. "And now, how about some dinner?"

"I never heard of anyone having dinner at six o'clock in the morning," I said.

"You've heard of it now," Jimmy said with a grin, and I walked into the mess hall with him. We had wonderful thick, juicy steaks, French fried potatoes and ice cream. Then Jimmy yawned.

"How about some shut-eye?" he said. "This has been a long day for you."

"Sure," I said sarcastically, "a long, tough day. How far did you fly tonight?"

"About fifteen hundred miles," Jimmy said.

"That's more than halfway from here to New York," I told him.

"That's a flight I wouldn't want to make." Jimmy Kenney shook his head. "All over water? Not me. This trip to Hamburg was easy compared to that."

"Do you think Sergeant Hannah would say it was easy?" I asked him.

"Sure he would," Jimmy said. And then he added, "Especially when he hears that I've recommended him for the Victoria Cross."

One of the other pilots had turned on the radio to get the 7:00 A.M. news. A voice said, "During the night, bombers of the RAF destroyed factories and other military targets in Hamburg, Germany. All of our aircraft returned safely."

Wing Commander Farmer grinned. "You almost spoiled our record, Jimmy," he said. "I've just been on the phone to headquarters, and I've got some news for you. They won't be able to replace your plane for three or four days, so if you want to, take forty-eight hours off."

"Why don't you come to London with me?" I suggested. "I can put you up in my apartment."

"I might as well," and Jimmy laughed. "I'm not of much use around here if they haven't got a plane for me to fly. What's it like in London these days?"

"You'll see, Jimmy, you'll see," I told him gravely.

CHAPTER 16

Bombs Over London at Night

WE DROVE TO LONDON THE NEXT DAY. HERE AND there we'd notice a whole block that had been destroyed by bombing, but London was still standing. The people were cheerful, and everybody went to his job every day just as he had before the bombing started. As soon as night came, the sirens sounded.

"What's that for?" Jimmy Kenney asked me curiously.

"That's the alert," I said. "That means the

German planes are on their way here. Didn't you ever hear an alert before?"

"I haven't been in London since the war began," he explained.

I took Jimmy to dinner, in a good restaurant three stories below the street surface, where it was very quiet. After dinner he was tired, so we went to bed. We fell asleep, but at three o'clock that morning Jimmy woke me up.

"How can you sleep, with bombs falling all around?" he wanted to know.

That puzzled me. When a bomb falls it makes a screaming sound that wakes you right up. But I couldn't hear any bombs falling. High above I could hear the drone of airplanes, and I could hear the London anti-aircraft guns blasting, but there were no bombs falling.

"Listen to them!" Jimmy said excitedly. "Sounds as though they're dropping right outside our windows."

Then I realized what was the matter. As he said, Jimmy Kenney hadn't been in London since the bombing began, and so he hadn't heard the city's nightly concerts.

"Listen, Jimmy," I explained patiently, "those aren't bombs you're hearing. They're anti-aircraft guns stationed in Hyde Park, just a couple of blocks from here."

"They're guns?" He was incredulous.

"You're a bomber pilot, Jimmy. How many bombs have you dropped in the past few months?"

"I don't know," he said. "Eight or nine hundred, I guess."

"And you don't even know the difference between the sound of a gun shooting up and a bomb coming down?"

"I never heard a bomb explode," he said miserably. "When we drop our bombs we're traveling fast. By the time they land and explode, we're four or five miles away. I just never heard a bomb explode."

"Well, stick around, Jimmy, you will! Now get back to sleep. I'll wake you up if a bomb drops."

The next night the Nazis really gave it to us hot and heavy in London. By then Jimmy knew everything about bombs—or thought he did. I woke him late that night after six bombs had dropped very close.

"We've had enough, Jimmy," I told him. "This apartment is on the eighth floor. We're too high up for comfort. Let's go down to the lobby until things quiet down."

Jimmy Kenney laughed. "They weren't bombs," he said. "They were guns—our guns. Can't you even tell the difference between a gun and a bomb?"

Just then a big one whistled down. It started very high, and we could follow its progress by the noise it made as it descended. It landed just at the back of my apartment house, and the whole building swayed. All our windows broke with a crash, and then the lights went out.

"Maybe you were right," Jimmy said. "Maybe they were bombs, at that."

The elevators weren't working, so we had to

walk down to the street. The cellar of the apartment house had been fixed up as a shelter, and just about everyone who lived in the house was down there.

During the first weeks of the bombing, no one bothered to go to shelters. But then, gradually, everyone realized that if they didn't go to a shelter they couldn't get any sleep. If they didn't get any sleep they wouldn't be much good at their offices the next day. So during a big raid every sensible person took a few blankets and went to a shelter to snatch some sleep.

On that particular night, at least sixty people had spread out on the floor of the apartment house cellar and were sound asleep. I saw an old friend of mine, named Sydney Wolf, who was a member of the House of Commons. (That is just like being a Congressman in the United States.) We joined him and I introduced him to Jimmy. Sydney Wolf looked worried, which surprised me, because I knew he was a very brave man.

"What are you worrying about, Sydney?" I asked him.

"I'll tell you," he said. "As you know, I own a farm just about thirty miles outside of London. I phoned my wife about an hour ago at the farm, and she told me that several bombs had dropped in that area."

"They didn't hit the farm, did they?" I asked.

"They didn't hit the house," he said, "but I'm worried about my cows. One bomb, my wife told me, knocked the doors off our barn, and our bull and our sixty cows ran out into the pasture."

"Are cows scared by bombs?" Jimmy Kenney asked.

"Yes," Sydney said gloomily, "and that's what I'm worried about. It's a strange thing, but when cows get scared they give sour milk. After a bombing they stay scared for about four days.

My wife told me we wouldn't have any good milk for some time from our cows."

"Do bombs scare a bull?" Jimmy asked.

"No," Sydney said. "Our bull always gets mad when he hears the bombs. And when that bull gets mad, he lowers his head and charges until he hits something. It's all right if he runs into a stack of hay, but I'm always afraid that he'll run into a tree. That bull cost us more than a hundred and fifty pounds, and I'd hate to have him kill himself."

"What other animals have you got on your farm?" Jimmy asked.

"We've got all kinds of animals," Sydney said. "We've got six farm horses, and they become very frightened when they hear the bombs. We have turkeys, too, and some of them have been scared to death. Dogs never get scared. I have four of them at the farm. When they hear German planes fly over us, they bark furiously at them. Our dogs really hate Germans. The most sensible animals of all are cats, I think. We have two big tomcats. As soon as they hear the German planes come over, they get up quietly and go right down to the cellar."

Sydney yawned. "Well, I've got to get to sleep," he said wearily. "Mr. Churchill is going to speak in the House of Commons in the morning, and I want to be there to hear him."

Jimmy and I tried to sleep, but couldn't.

"I don't see how the people of London can take it," he said. "I think we in the RAF have it a lot easier. When we're up there in the air, nobody can drop a bomb on us. I don't know why people don't get out of London."

"Not even the King and Queen have left London," I told him. "They're over at Buckingham Palace, just a few blocks from here, taking the same risk that everybody else in London takes. They say that the King has tried very hard to

make the Queen leave London, but she won't
go. She sent her two children to the country, but
she stays here. Someone wrote a nice little poem
to the Queen. It was in one of the London papers
the other day. Do you want to hear it?"

Jimmy nodded.

"It goes like this," I said:

London Bridge is falling down,
              My fair Lady,
Be it said to your renown
That you wore your gayest gown,
Your bravest smile—
And stayed in town,
When London Bridge was falling down,
              My fair Lady.

CHAPTER 17

Plymouth

EVERY NIGHT THE GERMAN RADIO WOULD TELL us gleefully of English cities that had been wiped out. These statements always turned out to be lies. But the RAF fighters couldn't stop all the German bombers from getting through, and many English cities were badly damaged.

For some reason the Germans attacked the city of Plymouth again and again. Every American knows that the *Mayflower* left Plymouth on its famous voyage to our country. The city is also renowned because it was from there that

Sir Francis Drake sailed so often to fight the Spanish fleet. When I heard that Plymouth had been bombed five nights in a row, I decided to see for myself how bad the damage was.

Plymouth had been hurt, all right. At the time I reached there, at least half of its 200,000 people were homeless.

Plymouth was a city of churches. However, its famous bells, like all the others in England, hadn't been heard since the Battle of Britain had started. The reason for this was that Winston Churchill had told all of the ministers and priests in England not to ring their church bells unless there was an invasion. Hitler had boasted that he would invade England. If his troops had ever crossed the Channel and landed on English soil, every church bell in England would have rung to warn the people.

While I was in Plymouth, I met the Mayor of

the city, Lord Astor, and he told me about the raids.

"If London can take it, I guess we can take it," he said calmly. "The Germans have been coming over for the last five nights, and they have done a lot of damage. In fact, the whole city would have burned to the ground if it hadn't been for Sir Francis Drake."

"Sir Francis Drake!" I exclaimed. "He's been dead for about three hundred and fifty years!"

"That's right," the Mayor said. "But back in 1580 he gave Plymouth its first reservoir. In addition to being a great admiral, Drake was a great engineer. He brought water here to Plymouth from Lake Burrator, just twelve miles away. He built a stone-lined trench, and the water of the lake flowed through it to the reservoir. About a hundred years ago the world learned that iron pipes could be used to bring water to a city, and so Plymouth no longer needed Drake's reservoir. But we have always kept it filled with water out of respect to Sir Francis Drake.

"Then two nights ago, when bombs destroyed our water mains and pipes, we ran out of water. All over the city, incendiary bombs had started fires and the firemen had no water to put them out. Suddenly I remembered the old reservoir, and told the firemen to pipe its water through their hose. They did, and Plymouth was saved. Drake, who has been dead for almost three hundred and fifty years, had come out of the past to save his home town."

"How are you feeding the people today?" I asked the Mayor.

"The Queen's Messengers are feeding them." He smiled. Kindhearted people in America had raised money to buy fifty big mobile canteens. They had been sent as a present to the Queen.

"Mobile canteens" were huge trucks which

contained stoves, big soup pots, and ovens for
baking bread. When a city was badly bombed,
these Queen's Messengers, as they were called,
rushed to the stricken city. The big trucks were
stationed all over Plymouth, and lines of hungry
men and women stretched in front of them.
There was no gas or electricity in Plymouth, and
no one could do any cooking. But the Queen's
Messengers were filled with vegetable soup, beef

stew, bread, and tea. Because of the kindness of American friends, no one in Plymouth went hungry.

As I walked around Plymouth, something seemed to be missing. For the longest time I couldn't figure out what it was—and then suddenly it came over me that I hadn't heard any children. I hadn't heard any children crying. I hadn't seen any children playing. In fact, I hadn't seen any children at all. I asked the Mayor what had happened to them.

"Today Plymouth is a city without children," he said. "As soon as the bombings began we decided to send our children away. We put up tents in the fields outside the city, and moved all the children there. Nurses are taking care of them."

The Mayor took me to the waterfront to show me a tablet which marked the spot where the Pilgrims started out aboard the *Mayflower* in

1620. They sailed to Plymouth, Massachusetts, and landed on the famous Plymouth Rock. Everything around the tablet had been bombed into rubble, but the tablet remained untouched.

"The German planes will come again and again," the Mayor said, "and many of us will die, but Plymouth will survive. We really believe that old Francis Drake is taking care of us, just as he protected England long ago from the 'Dons,' as he called the Spaniards. Every school child in Plymouth learns the famous poem about Drake written by Sir Henry Newbolt. It tells of his death aboard his ship, which was then cruising in the West Indies. The poem supposedly gives an account of his last words and they show that even in a distant land he was thinking of Plymouth in the County of Devon. The poem is called 'Drake's Drum,' and part of it goes like this:

Take my drum to England, hang it by the shore,
strike it when your powder's running low.
If the Dons sight Devon, I'll quit the port of
Heaven and we'll drum them up the Channel
as we drummed them long ago.

"We really believe," the Mayor told me earnestly, "that when Plymouth is in danger, Drake strikes his drum. Every man, woman, and child who was in Plymouth on the first night of the blitz last week will tell you they heard the drum even before we heard the German planes. The drum told us to fight on and never give up. And we never will."

Her buildings were ruined, her churches in ashes, her streets filled with rubble, her shops and stores masses of debris, but Plymouth was still very much alive. When the Germans said that they had destroyed Plymouth, they were very much mistaken. Plymouth, I knew, would be saved. I wasn't so sure that Drake would save it, but I was sure that the RAF would.

CHAPTER 18

A City of Caves

LORD ASTOR HAD SAID THAT LONDON COULD take it. When I returned to the city, I was aware more than ever of the truth of his statement. London had become a city of caves. Every afternoon as soon as the dusk came, the siren wailed to give warning that the German bombers were on their way. Families of Londoners walked to the nearest subway station, with mothers carrying milk for babies and thermos bottles of hot tea. They brought toys for the children and they brought their pets—dogs and cats.

The subway stations far below the streets were the safest places to be during the nightly air raids. Mothers would bring blankets and lay them on the subway platform, and then settle down for a long wait. Down there they couldn't hear the drone of the German bombers, but when the bombs screamed down they could be heard, all right. The exploding bombs added to the noise, and if they landed close, the subway platforms trembled.

The subways were very crowded, but no one minded. Sometimes a baby cried, but I never saw fear on the faces of even the smallest children. And always there was someone in the crowd with an accordion or a harmonica. He would play "There'll Always Be an England," or "Tomorrow Is a Lovely Day," and everyone would sing. Sometimes the singing would drown out the noise of the guns which were firing at the planes high above. But the singing never

drowned out the sound of the bombs that landed.

At nine o'clock at night everyone quieted down in the subway stations and in the shelters. Fathers and mothers had to be at work in the morning and they needed their sleep. When a subway train pulled into a station, the people asleep on the platforms never woke up—they were used to the noise, and hardly heard the trains. At least half of the city's population slept in subway stations or cellars. The other half were out in the streets protecting the city as best they could.

Twenty thousand of these people were air wardens. They patrolled the streets and reported fires. They ran into burning buildings to pull people out of them. They gave first aid to the wounded and summoned ambulances and firemen. The ambulances were driven by girls, some of them only eighteen or nineteen. No matter how many bombs were falling, they drove their ambulances through the streets to wherever they were needed.

Another twenty thousand people were firemen who were on duty in London every night. They weren't regular firemen; they were men who worked all day in offices or factories, but who worked as firemen every night. All night long the fire engines went screaming through the streets, and we would know that some part of London was on fire. Half the city worked at night so the other half could sleep.

Thousands of people crowded into the cellars of apartment houses and hotels, for the subways couldn't hold everyone. The hotels had very comfortable underground shelters. Each hotel had fixed up its cellar as a first-aid station. Doctors and nurses were on duty all night. Sometimes when a hospital was hit the ambulance drivers brought their wounded to the hotels.

One of London's biggest hotels is called Claridge's. One night during a bad air raid I entered the hotel and went downstairs to the shelter where I knew hot tea and coffee were always on hand. At least two thousand army cots had been put up in the cellar, and people were asleep on every cot. At one table a girl was serving hot drinks. I asked her for a cup of coffee.

"Of course," she said cheerfully, pouring it out.

I started talking to her, but she held her finger to her lips. "Be quiet," she whispered, "you'll wake up the Queen."

"What Queen?" I asked.

"Queen Wilhelmina of Holland," she said. "She's asleep on that cot over there." And sure enough, she was.

Queens and waiters, businessmen and factory workers, policemen and teachers faced the same uncertainties at night, when the German planes were overhead. England was proving that she was a real democracy, all right. Everyone ate the same food, had the same ration of sugar and tea, and everyone shared the same danger.

While I was drinking my coffee I heard a little whimper. I looked around, and there, tied to one of the cots, was a dog—a light-brown cocker spaniel. The dog noticed me and wagged his tail. The owner of the dog was asleep on the cot.

"The puppy wants to go out," the girl who was serving the coffee said.

As I walked over to the dog, he looked up at me with his big friendly eyes and wagged his tail.

"You want to go out, pup?" I asked, and the little dog started to bark with excitement. I untied his leash and led him up to the lobby. He tugged at the leash and pulled me outside into the dark street. It was very noisy because of the anti-aircraft guns at Hyde Park, not far from the hotel, but the cocker spaniel didn't seem to mind it. He just loved being out in the fresh air. He didn't care about guns or bombs; he wanted to have his nightly walk.

I walked him around the block and he had a wonderful time. Just as we reached the hotel, a bomb fell only a couple of blocks away. It scared me, but it didn't scare the dog. He merely growled and then barked angrily.

I thought we'd both be better off in the underground shelter, so I brought the dog down into the cellar. The girl who was serving the coffee give him a cracker. He ate it and then sat up and begged for more.

"This little dog doesn't know there's a war on," the girl said, laughing.

"He's the only one in London who doesn't know it," I said. "Even the animals at the zoo know there's a war on."

During the blitz most of the animals were moved out of the London zoo. It had been a wonderful zoo, but those in charge were afraid that the repercussion from the bombs might blast open the cages, resulting in the animals' finding themselves loose. So the lions and the elephants were moved to Scotland. The snakes and the camels and the monkeys were sent to safer zoos. But the bears stayed right where they were.

The bears in the London zoo lived not in cages but in caves. The keepers noticed that as soon as the German bombers came over the bears would look up at the sky and then walk calmly into their caves, where they would be safe. Lots of bombs fell on the London zoo, but not a single bear was ever hit.

"Bears are smarter than humans," the head keeper told me. "Some humans haven't got sense enough to come in out of the rain or in out of a bombing. You never see a bear standing out in the rain and you never see a bear outside when the bombs start coming down."

CHAPTER 19

England Could Take It

In OCTOBER, 1940, THE GERMAN AIR FORCE came over London every night. And every night the RAF night fighters were up there knocking them down. Still the Germans came. Several times it seemed as if they had sent the whole Luftwaffe at London.

I happened to be at the Hotel Savoy during one of the major raids in October, with a number of other American war correspondents. During the air attack, I left the hotel, which is on the banks of the Thames, and walked outdoors to see what was happening. So many fires had been started that it appeared to be daylight.

Across the Thames was a long line of warehouses. All of them were in flames, and I could see the fire engines over there with their hose trained on the fires. As the water from the hose met the flames, a great hissing could be heard.

High above I could hear the uneven drone of what sounded like hundreds of German bombers.

Another war correspondent and I went up to the roof of the hotel. The German planes were dropping incendiaries, which were causing fires to spring up all over, as well as big block-busters. The night was filled with noise—all of it frightening noise.

From the roof we could see the whole city of London spread out before us. London was really on fire that night. The anti-aircraft guns were firing, and when they exploded, bright gold and

purple flashes could be seen in the sky. Now and
then there would be a big bright white flash,
and we would know that a German bomber had
been hit.

Whatever goes up must come down. So, before long, fragments of the shells which were bursting five miles up in the sky started to rain down on the roof of the hotel. I returned to the safety of the hotel lobby below.

In a little while two American press correspondents, George Lait of International News Service, and Merrill "Red" Mueller of National Broadcasting Company, walked in. Their clothes were ripped and their faces were black with soot.

It didn't take George and Red long to tell their story. Three bombs had landed in the street on which they lived (about a mile from the hotel), setting fire to all the houses on the block. Lait and Mueller had worked with the firemen and air wardens, pulling out the wounded from the burning buildings.

George Lait said, "We knew the family next door to us very well. They had a little girl who was three years old. We knew they all slept in the cellar of their house, so Red and I rushed in there to see if they were all right. The smoke was so thick we couldn't breathe, but we smashed a couple of windows and let some air in. The mother and father were lying there as though they were asleep, but they were both suffocated from the smoke."

"We thought the little girl was still alive," Red Mueller said. "We carried her out into the street and gave her artificial respiration for an hour. Then a doctor examined her and said it was too late."

"Maybe she's better off dead," I said, thinking how hard life would have been for the little girl if she had lived as an orphan.

George Lait shook his head. "Nobody's better off dead," he said.

Several times the big Savoy Hotel shook under the fury of the bombs. The telephones weren't working by that time, but the radio was. The radio warned everybody to be calm and to use as little water as possible. The firemen needed all the water they could get to keep the flames from spreading.

At 4:00 A.M. the dawn came, and the sirens sounded the "All Clear." All of us who loved London felt very sad. We knew that London had been horribly hurt during the night. Had her great heart stopped beating?

I walked out into the streets. They were filled with grim-faced men and women, but there was no fear on their faces. Just a block from the Savoy I saw the smoking wreckage of the famous Church of St. Clements. This is one of the oldest churches in London, famous for its wonderful bells. Every school child in London knows the nursery rhyme which begins,

Oranges and lemons,
Say the bells of St. Clements.

I walked down to see if the House of Commons had been hit. It had been.

It was a warm, sunny morning, but a heavy pall of smoke hung over the city. Smoke was coming from the House of Commons, and as I watched, an automobile drew up and two men got out. One was Winston Churchill and the other Anthony Eden. They went into the House of Commons to inspect the damage. When they came out a few minutes later, Mr. Churchill had a cigar clamped between his teeth. His face was filled with anger.

"We'll make them pay for this," I heard him say to Anthony Eden.

Just opposite the House of Commons was the famous Westminster Abbey. It too had been hit. In the square facing the House and Westminster Abbey there was a huge statue of Abraham Lincoln. It was comforting to see the strong face of Lincoln there that morning. Probably he understood why the Germans had bombed the House of Commons and Westminster Abbey. The Germans thought of them as military targets. The House of Commons in England is the symbol of free speech. Westminster Abbey has always been the symbol of faith. Germany had declared war on free speech and on faith. That's why they had bombed the House of Commons and Westminster Abbey.

I walked back to the hotel. Gradually the firemen were getting the blaze under control. They were clearing the debris from the streets. Back at the hotel there was a message that all press correspondents were to report to RAF Headquarters.

We all walked to the big building about ten blocks away, expecting to hear nothing but gloomy news. We knew that at least four of London's railroad stations had been badly bombed. We knew that three of the newspaper buildings had been hit. We knew that at least a dozen warehouses across the Thames had been destroyed. We assembled in the big conference room and then an Air Marshal (who is equivalent to a General in our Air Force) walked briskly into the room.

"I'm sorry to have called you here so early," he said, and to our surprise he was smiling. "I know nobody in London got any sleep during the night. But I have a very important announcement to make, especially to you American correspondents. Last night," he said solemnly, "London was hurt badly. You know that. But what you don't know is this. I believe we have at last won the Battle of Britain."

CHAPTER 20

The Battle Is Won

WE ALL LOOKED IN AMAZEMENT AT THE AIR Marshal, whose name was Harris. Many of us felt that the Battle of Britain had been lost the night before. Now he was saying that the Battle had been won. What made him think so? He smiled and went on.

"We have always said that if we were able to destroy ten per cent of an attacking air force, we could in time destroy that whole air force. No air force can afford to lose more than ten per cent of its airplanes and crews in an attack. German losses have been increasing steadily un-

til in a number of raids we have destroyed more than ten per cent of their planes. As a result of increased defense on our part, the raids have become both less frequent and less intense. We now feel that the Battle of Britain has been won."

"How about London?" one of the press correspondents asked the Air Marshal.

"London is something like your American heavyweight champion, Joe Louis," he said with a smile. "Sometimes Joe Louis gets knocked down; sometimes he gets hurt; but no one can keep him on the floor. And when he is hurt he fights back all the harder. London is like that. Within two hours from now trains will be coming in and going out of London as usual. Within two hours from now every fire will be out and every water main repaired."

"Air Marshal," a correspondent said, "the Battle of Britain began on August 8th. On that date the Germans boasted they had ten thousand bomber and fighter planes ready to hurl against England. How many planes has the RAF destroyed?"

"I have the figures right here," Air Marshal Harris said. "Since August 8th, Germany lost

2,375 planes in her daylight raids. Since her
night raids began she has lost another nine hundred planes. That is a total of 3,275 German
airplanes which have been destroyed. At least
another five hundred were so badly damaged
that we won't have to worry about them."

"How many planes has the RAF lost?" another press correspondent asked.

"We have lost 375 fighter planes and sixty
bombers, a total of 435 planes," he said. "We
don't care about the planes, but we are saddened
because of the pilots who have been killed. We
have had to pay a high price, but we have won
the Battle of Britain and saved England. Every
day your wonderful American airplanes arrive
here in greater numbers. Because of them we
will now be able to give Berlin and every other
German city a taste of what the people of London have been going through."

In time the world learned that everything the

Air Marshal had said was true. Nor has it forgotten the memorable address made by Winston Churchill. He gave full credit to the RAF for saving England, ending his tribute with these words, which became famous: "Never in the field of human conflict was so much owed by so many to so few."

CHAPTER 21

Hope for the Future

THE BATTLE OF BRITAIN BEGAN ON AUGUST 8, 1940, and ended on October 31, 1940. It had lasted eighty-four days. America was not yet in the war and would not be for another year and five weeks. But she had helped enormously with her fine airplanes and her guns and ammunition.

In London we still weren't certain that the Battle of Britain was over. However, the raids grew smaller and smaller until we finally did realize that the first great air battle of the war had come to an end. Hitler had thrown every-

Winston Churchill

thing he had at England, but England was still standing and she was growing stronger every day.

Although we knew there would be other long and dreadful battles on land, in the air, and at sea, people in England no longer worried about what would happen. America was their strong-hearted ally, and America was sending more and more materiel every week. England no longer felt as though she were standing alone. She had taken Hitler's hardest punch, had been knocked down, but had gotten up before the count of nine. Oh, England had been hurt, all right.

During the eighty-four days of the Battle of Britain, 12,581 men, women, and children had been killed and 16,965 had been injured. In London German bombs had destroyed a hundred docks, and had ruined hundreds of homes and factories. Bombs had even fallen on Buckingham Palace. Cities like Coventry and Plymouth and Liverpool had been hit badly, but now they could get ready for the second round. It would come in the spring—everyone knew that. But everyone faced it with confidence. Churchill looked more like a bulldog than ever; he smiled, growled like a bulldog, and the people still loved him.

Index

ASDIC. *See* Anti-submarine detection

A-20A (plane), 82

Air wardens, 155

Airfield (s), 52-53, 83-84

Alert (siren), 133-34

Ambulances, 155

American boys. *See* Eagle Squadron

Anti-aircraft fire and guns, 14-15, 18, 40-41, 43, 108, 112, 117, 127-28, 135, 158, 162

Anti-submarine detection, 41-42, 45, 48

Arsenal (code name), 118

Astor, Lord, 145-50, 152

Biggin Hill Airport, 25, 56-64, 73-74, 80, 85

Boston (plane), 102

Boulogne, France, 43

Brighton, England, 96-97

Brighton (ship), 14

Britain (Battle of), 9-13, 52, 102, 108, 144, 169, 170-73, 175, 177

British Navy. *See* Royal Navy

Brown, Albert, 54-56, 60-64, 65-66, 69, 70, 73-74, 79, 82, 84-85

Buckingham Palace, 141-42, 177

Burrator (lake), 145

Bacon convoy (code name), 25, 30

Bader, Douglas, 10-11

Bears, 160

C-Squadron, 79

Calais, France, 26, 28, 30, 32-34, 43, 89-90

Canteens, 146-47

Children, 148, 177
Church bells, 144
Churchill, Winston, 107-08, 141, 144, 167, 174, 177
Claridge's (hotel), London, 156-57
Coen, Oscar, 80
Commons, House of, 167-68
Convoys, 13-14, 17-18, 20, 25-28, 31-33, 37, 106
Coventry, England, 105, 177
Crowley, Jimmy, 78-79

Daniels, Danny, 80
Daymond, Gus, 78-80
Democracy, 157
Douglas, Arthur, 56-62, 67-71
Dover, England, 28-30, 40, 70
"Downing a plane," 67-68
Drake, Sir Francis, 144-46, 149-51
"Drake's Drum," *poem* (Newboldt), 149-50

E-boat (s), 35-36, 46, 48
Eagle Squadron, 75-81
Eden, Anthony, 167
Ederle, Gertrude, 29
Edgerton, Jack, 97
England, 3-11; airfields, 52-53; aloneness, 6; bombing, 105, 143; cities, 143; "could take it," 161-69; population, 4; size, 3-4
English Channel, 9, 11, 13-15, 20, 23-24, 29-30, 40, 44, 49, 55, 60, 87-88, 93-94, 97, 106-07, 144, 150
English Navy. *See* Royal Navy

Farmer, Rod, 114-15, 116-18, 120-24, 127, 131
Festler, Jack, 80
Firemen, 155-56
Flak. See Anti-aircraft fire
Folkestone, England, 61, 67
Football, 38, 55, 61
France, 6, 107

Geiger, Bill, 80
German Air Force. See *Luftwaffe*
Germany, 107-08, 111, 113, 115
Goering, Hermann, 8

Hall, Bill, 80
Hamburg, Germany, 109-18, 131
Ham-handed pilots, 99
Hannah, Sergeant, 125-31
Harris (air marshal), 170-72

Heinkels, 21, 22-28, 63-64, 67-68

Hitler, Adolf, 5-7, 13, 144, 175-76

Holland, 107

Hooper, Richard, 85-90, 91-96, 98-104

Hudsons (bombers), 107

Hurricanes, 8-11, 52, 54

*I*ntruders, 82-90

Isotta-Fraschini motors, 36

Kenney, James, 108-15, 117-24, 125-38, 141, 142

Kirk, Bill, 15

Lait, George, 164-65

Lancasters (bombers), 108

Le Bourget (airport), 92

Lincoln, Abraham, *statue,* 167-68

Liverpool, England, 98, 105, 177

London, England, 52-53, 68-69, 76, 98-104, 105-06, 108, 132, 133-42, 145, 152-60, 161-69, 172-73, 175, 177

"London Bridge was falling down" (poem), 142

London Zoo, 159-60

Lord Haw-Haw (broadcast), 51

Louis, Joe, 172

Luftwaffen, 5-10, 13, 51, 52-53, 63, 108, 161, 172-73

MTB. *See* Motor torpedo boats

Mamedoff, Andy, 80

Mayflower (ship), 143, 148-49

ME-*109,* 63

ME-*110,* 63

Messerschmitt, 59, 63, 67-68

Mohawks (planes), 107

Motor torpedo boats, 46-48

Mueller, Merrill, 164-65

Newboldt, Sir Henry, 149-50

Owen (squadron leader), 117

P-37's, 107

P-40's, 107

Paris, France, 90-91

Peterson, Gordon, 78-80

Piper Cubs, 76-77

Plane crash, confirmation, 67-68

Plymouth, England, 105, 143-51, 177

Pompey. *See* Portsmouth

Portsmouth, England, 12-14, 49-51

Queen's Messengers, 146-47

RAF. *See* Royal Air Force

Radar, 35-36, 39, 55, 89, 100

Radio, 25, 32, 38-39, 66, 84, 89, 117-18, 122, 165-66

Roosevelt, Franklin D., 107

Royal Air Force, 8-11, 26, 36, 39, 42-43, 50, 52, 57, 65-72, 75-80, 91-92, 105-15, 161, 168, 172-73; Churchill tribute, 174

Royal Navy, 4-5, 38

Saint Clements Church, London, 166

Savoy Hotel, London, 161-62, 164-66

Scotland, 159

"Scramble," 57, 59

Simpson, Peter, 15, 17-21

Smoke, use of, 46-49

Soccer, 38, 55

Spitfire (s) 8-9, 18-19, 22-28, 32, 39, 49, 51, 52, 55, 56, 60, 62-63, 66, 69, 74, 77-78, 102-04

"Stick," 57, 99

Submarines, 46, 48

Subway stations, 153-55

Thames River, 100-01, 161-62

Tobin, Gene (Red), 76-78, 80-81

Tomahawks (planes), 107

"Walkie-Talkie," 62

Ward room, 24, 38

Westminster Abbey, 167-68

Whitleys (bombers), 108, 109

Wilhelm, Kaiser, 7-8

Wilhelmina, Queen, 157

Wing commander, 54

Wolf, Sydney, 138-41

World War I, 7-8